Eɪ

"The girl's guide to armored living! I love the way that Sharon Norris Elliott speaks eternal and unchangeable truth in new words. Just when you think you've heard all there is to hear about the spiritual armor, here comes *Power Suit*. I highly recommend it."
—**Jennifer Kennedy Dean**, best-selling author of *Live a Praying Life*

"'Get up, get dressed, get going, and start winning!' Wise words from a wise woman. In her latest book, *Power Suit,* Sharon shows us how to take responsibility for dressing appropriately for the battles we face every day. This is a must-read for every woman who wants to win those battles!"
—**Florence Littauer**, international author and speaker

"Sharon has hit a home run again! She takes the passage about the armor of God and makes it clear, practical, and relevant. I love Sharon's use of Scripture, story, and interesting detail to make the passage come alive. You'll never get dressed again without thinking of God's empowering Power Suit protecting your heart and mind."
—**Kathy Collard Miller**, conference speaker and author of *Women of the Bible* ("The Smart Guide to the Bible" Series)

"Sharon is one of my favorite authors and speakers combining her warm wit and wisdom to timely topics."
—**James N. Watkins**, award-winning author and speaker

Tanya,
Get dressed!

love,
Sharon Elliott

POWER
SUIT

SHARON
NORRIS ELLIOTT

POWER
SUIT

The ARMOR of GOD
FIT for the FEMININE FRAME

NEW HOPE
PUBLISHERS
Birmingham, Alabama

New Hope® Publishers
P. O. Box 12065
Birmingham, AL 35202-2065
www.newhopepublishers.com
New Hope Publishers is a division of WMU®.

Library of Congress Cataloging-in-Publication Data

Elliott, Sharon Norris, 1957-
  Power suit : the armor of God fit for the feminine frame / Sharon Norris Elliott.
    p. cm.
  ISBN 978-1-59669-238-1 (sc)
  1. Christian women--Religious life. I. Title.
  BV4527.E446 2011
  248.8'43--dc22
                                    2010047147

All Scripture quotations unless otherwise noted are taken from the HOLY BIBLE, NEW INTERNATIONAL VERSION®. NIV®. Copyright©1973, 1978, 1984 by International Bible Society. Used by permission of Zondervan. All rights reserved.

Scripture quotations marked KJV are taken from The Holy Bible, King James Version.

Scripture quotations marked NASB are taken from the New American Standard Bible®, Copyright © 1960, 1962, 1963, 1968, 1971, 1972, 1973, 1975, 1977, 1995 by The Lockman Foundation. Used by permission.

Scripture quotations marked NLT are taken from the *Holy Bible*, New Living Translation, copyright © 1996. Used by permission of Tyndale House Publishers, Inc., Wheaton, Illinois. All rights reserved.

Scripture quotations marked NKJV are taken from the New King James Version. Copyright © 1982 by Thomas Nelson, Inc. Used by permission. All rights reserved.

ISBN-10: 1-59669-238-3
ISBN-13: 978-1-59669-238-1

N094135 • 0311 • 3M1

Have you heard of the armor of God—and attempted to implement it?

We can find ourselves down more than up...shaking our heads, wondering what hit us. The armor doesn't seem to be working as it should.

Our defeats in spiritual battles are not because of any defect in the Power Suit, but because of problems with the fit.

—Sharon

Dedication

This book is dedicated to my mother,

Nancy J. Norris.

She passed into glory before she saw any of my books published,
But she was the power that bore me,
Nourished me,
Believed in me,
And let me know that
If I trusted and prayed like everything depended on God,
And worked like everything depended on me,
I could accomplish absolutely anything.

She wore the Power Suit
With quiet dignity
Every day.

I love her,
Thank her,
And am confident
That we will spend eternity
In God's presence together.

Table of Contents

Introduction

While writing this book, whenever I told people the topic, they would inevitably respond, "Oh, so you're writing a book about spiritual warfare."

I guess that's true. A book discussing armor probably mentions warfare, but I didn't think of the topic in the light of spiritual warfare until folks kept saying that's what I was writing about. When I think about spiritual warfare, my mind conjures up visions of angels and demons battling over issues pertaining to us saints. I see a tug-of-war over one man's decision to remain faithful to his wife or not. Further away on the field, one hears the clash of spiritual swords over a woman's attitude toward her underqualified yet cocky boss. Then I envision hand-to-hand combat regarding a young adult's thoughts on the practicality, possibility, and purpose of maintaining his sexual purity. All the while in the background is the insistent drone of Satan's nasty voice as he boldly screams accusations against the people of God in an effort to move God toward our abandonment.

All of that makes for an exciting Hollywood action scene, but spiritual warfare—although as intense in motive—is covertly conniving. We would be more guarded if the enemy of our souls attacked straight on. Yet, this wily sucker has deceived people throughout the ages by approaching us with smooth talk and easy answers. A line from an old Keith Green song depicts Satan's sentiment: "I used to have to sneak around, but now they just open their doors. It's getting very easy now, 'cause no one believes in me anymore."

Yes, instead of the action-packed scene depicted above, the spiritual battle we're in is more like guerilla warfare. There are no rules and no one follows the Geneva Convention. Satan is not an officer and a gentleman. He and his demonic hordes stealthily slither around the saints of God, patiently waiting for a convenient opening—a weak spot at which to strike.

This book seeks to bring the battle out into the open. Contrary to popular belief, what you don't know can most definitely hurt you. These pages hope to bring to light the everydayness of the battles being fought in the spiritual realm. The big problems exist: serious illnesses, depression, oppression, death, and so on, but the little foxes spoil the vine (Song of Solomon 2:15; 2 Peter 2:1–3). We spend so much time worrying about and preparing for the big bombs to be dropped, we ignore the fact that we're walking through minefields. We are losing battles in our Christian lives daily, and it's our own fault. We're being trained, but we're not properly outfitted.

Join me in the dressing room as I help you put on your Power Suit—the armor of God fit for the feminine frame.

Section 1
Perspective and Truth

Chapter 1

The Power Suit Perspective

Fit for You

You drop by your favorite department store to pick up one item—the facial cleanser you ran out of this morning. You intend to run in, make your purchase, and run back out. But on entering, your eye catches the colorful banners announcing the "Half Yearly Sale." How in the world could you have forgotten? *This is the best sale of the season! Miss it now, and it's another six-month wait.*

OK, you tell yourself, *I'll give myself just 20 minutes to take a quick look around. Then I'll make a beeline to the cosmetics for my cleanser and be back in the car in a flash.*

As soon as you enter your favorite department, there it is—a rack of classy business suits (or insert your particular weakness here), exactly like the ones in the catalogs you've been drooling over all season. You pick one up. Silk blend, designer label. It's not only practical and the right color, it's 70 percent off. Bingo! This puppy is calling your name.

There's just one tiny problem: You didn't leave the house in shopping mode. You're not dressed for ease of changing in the dressing room. You're wearing button-up jeans with tennis shoes that need to be untied to be removed, not to mention your pullover sweatshirt and T-shirt underneath. This is going to be tricky.

No problem, you decide. *I'll just slip it on over my clothes. No need to button or zip up. After a couple of turns, I'll be able to tell if it fits.*

The wait for an open dressing room pushes you close to that 20-minute promise you made to yourself, but you carry out your plan. Bulk and all, you eye the beautiful suit as your old clothes bunch and bulge under its finery. You don't really know how that suit looks on you. You don't know if you'll need a different undergarment. You're not sure about the waistband or the fit at the shoulders. Even though in reality you look a mess, you decide to make the purchase.

Does this description sound a bit ridiculous? All too often, we play out this same scenario with much more important "clothing" than sale suits. We strut around masquerading in godly values like truth, righteousness, and peace, all the while "wearing" them over hearts filled with deception, sin, and discord. And believe me; people can see the bulky junk poking through.

God has provided a spiritual suit of clothes that can, indeed, indicate the actual heart and life-attitude of the wearer. This suit even comes with protection so much better than Scotchgard™ that not only the suit but the one wearing the suit is shielded in many ways. You can have one exactly your size, but in order for it to fit properly to afford you the maximum benefit, you're first going to have to get rid of the other stuff you're wearing. A designer double-breasted tweed blazer with a matching knee-length skirt and perfect silk blouse will probably impress the higher-ups in the board room, your colleagues, and anyone passing by, but just wait until you wear the ultimate Power Suit God has designed. His "catalog" describes it this way:

Finally, be strong in the Lord and in his mighty power. Put on the full armor of God so that you can take your stand against the devil's schemes. For our struggle is not against flesh and blood, but against the rulers, against the authorities, against the powers of this dark world and against the spiritual forces of evil in the heavenly realms. Therefore put on the full armor of God, so that when the day of evil comes, you may be able to stand your ground, and after you have done everything, to stand. Stand firm then, with the belt of truth buckled around your waist, with the breastplate of righteousness in place, and with your feet fitted with the readiness that comes from the gospel of peace. In addition to all this, take up the shield of faith, with which you can extinguish all the flaming arrows of the evil one. Take the helmet of salvation and the sword of the Spirit, which is the word of God. And pray in the Spirit on all occasions with all kinds of prayers and requests. With this in mind, be alert and always keep on praying for all the saints (Ephesians 6:10–18).

Every type of clothing is designed to be worn a specific way. Take jeans, for example. You have low-rise, boot-cut, baggy, and tapered fits, to name a few. Low-rise jeans are intended to be worn in such a way that the waistband hits just below the belly button. This fit enables the wearer to show off her nicely indented waist. With boot-cut jeans, you can wear your boots, of course, or heavier shoes. Tapered jeans fit your figure, reach your waist, and are worn with a belt, while baggy jeans are intended to leave lots of room.

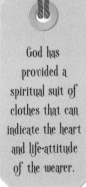

God has provided a spiritual suit of clothes that can indicate the heart and life-attitude of the wearer.

Fashion designers have catered to our every jean-wearing whim, while bolstering the underwear industry at the same time. Each style of jean requires a different style of undergarment as well. Low-rise jeans require low-rise undies, but baggy jeans are supposed to be worn with boxers underneath, intended to show. Tapered-fit jeans require some undergarment that won't show a line, while

The Power Suit Perspective   23

boot-cuts may also be low-rise, and you have to decide what would be best underneath. Let's not even get into color choice and whether you want your jeans regular or stretch denim (my personal favorite). Decisions, decisions, decisions—and all over jeans.

Well, leave it to our heavenly Father to uncomplicate the matter when it comes to our spiritual clothing. God's Power Suit adorns the spiritual woman inside of you and is meant to be worn with only the parts indicated. Putting on or leaving on your own stuff underneath destroys the whole effect.

This book will expose the carnal, secular, unspiritual, and ungodly "garments" we have on that will prevent the proper fit of the Power Suit. You will see how refusal to strip off those garments is keeping your Power Suit from fitting properly, and because of the poor fit, your spiritual life is not fully covered and protected. Our lives are kept by Christ; yet, God has made provision for us to clothe ourselves in His Power Suit, His all-powerful protection.

But before we get into exposing what we may already have on, let's look more closely at the catalog description of the Power Suit.

The Intention of the Power Suit

The purpose of the Power Suit is to supply us with strength. *"Be strong in the Lord and in his mighty power"* (Ephesians 6:10). Those words, *be strong* and *mighty power,* carry with them the idea of being empowered as we stand in relation to the source of power. In other words, the One who controls our life has the power (*kratos* [KRAH-tahss], meaning with flavors of power and strength), and we are drawing on His might (*ischus* [iss-KOOS], meaning ability and forcefulness).

My big brother, Nicholas Norris, was a career marine. Since there are 14 years between us, by the time I started kindergarten, he was already away in the service. However, even though he wasn't physically around, I knew my brother existed, and I knew that nobody messed with the marines. I knew my big brother loved me and would take care of me if need be. If anybody fooled with me, at five years old, I had somehow developed the secure notion that I had not only Nick, but the power of the entire United States Marine Corps behind me. My relationship with my brother (and by extension, in my mind, with the entire Marine Corps) empowered me.

God is telling us that our relationship to Him empowers us. We have all the arsenal of heaven at our disposal as long as we're suited up. The obvious deduction is, if we're being told to wear a suit for power, we must not already have the power this suit provides. And if God is telling us to suit up for power, there must be conflict coming. It would be utterly ridiculous for us to put on this suit for no reason. God does not require anything unnecessary.

We have all the arsenal of heaven at our disposal as long as we're suited up.

You may be thinking: *OK, so now I'm scared. What's God got in mind? What is He going to allow to come my way?*

I don't know. But I *do* know the wisdom of the saying "to be forewarned is to be forearmed." Don't be scared; be prepared. Life is going to happen to all of us, but thank God, He has made the power provision, and He does give us two good reasons we need it.

First, we have an enemy. The mass murderer, the devil, stalks us spiritually. God clearly tells us to wear the Power Suit *"so that you can take your stand against the devil's schemes"* (Ephesians 6:11). The word *schemes* is translated wiles in the King James Version, and means "trickery or to lie in wait." The Greek word *methodeia* [meth-thaw-DAY-uh] is the word from which we get our English word *methodology*. We need protection not only against the person of the devil, but also against his methodologies, the way he operates.

My husband and I enjoy watching crime dramas on television. From our armchairs, we participate with the law enforcement agents as they try to track down the bad guys. Inevitably, the officers are trying to figure out how the criminal thinks. If they can do that, they can anticipate his next move and apprehend him. James and I are getting pretty good at guessing the identity of the perpetrator before the shows even end, because we watch and listen for the clues the shows give us about how the perps operate.

God knows how Satan operates. We don't have to spend a lot of time investigating and expending extra energy questioning the process. God tells us straight out that Satan's scandalous methodology exists to destroy us, and He gives us power to stand against it.

I hear you thinking again: *But I don't intend to engage the devil in conflict. I'm not called to a ministry dealing with demons. Why can't I simply avoid contact with the devil, get out of his way, and go about my own business in my own clothes?*

God answers this question with the second reason for the Power Suit:

For our struggle is not against flesh and blood, but against the rulers, against the authorities, against the powers of this dark world and against the spiritual forces of evil in the heavenly realms. Therefore put on the full armor of God, so that when the day of evil comes, you may be able to stand your ground, and after you have done everything, to stand (Ephesians 6:12–13).

The struggle exists whether we want it or not. We may not be looking for Satan, but as Christians, we had better believe trouble is looking for us. In fact, we are in his cross hairs. God warns us, *"Be self-controlled and alert. Your enemy the devil prowls around like a roaring lion looking for someone to devour"* (1 Peter 5:8). This verse and Ephesians 6:12–13 are in the *present* tense. The struggle is present, ongoing, and spiritual in its essence.

So we'll face the struggle whether we want to or not. We must be always ready.

Ron, a police officer friend of ours, wears his bulletproof vest when he works in the streets. He's one of the many great officers in our city. His job is to protect and serve, and he never leaves his house for work looking to start trouble. However, perpetrators leave their houses every day looking to start trouble with him. Sometimes those bad guys have it in specifically for the officers, so Ron wears his vest.

The Operation of the Power Suit

OK, you say to yourself, *so I'm convinced of the need for this Power Suit, but exactly how does it work? How is it that I get this strength?*

I'm glad you asked. The passage makes it simple; put the suit on.

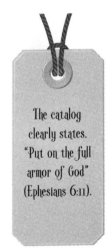

I do not have the power to fly, but if I were to put on an operating jet pack, I could. If I refused to put on the straps that attach it to my body, or neglected to fill the jet pack with the necessary fuel, I wouldn't get the benefit. If I decided not to take up the controls, I'd be grounded. In order to fly, I would have to appropriate everything about the jet pack that promised to get me into the air. Then, even as I soared above the earth, the power wouldn't be in me; it would be in the jet pack.

The catalog clearly states. "Put on the full armor of God" (Ephesians 6:11).

So it is with the Power Suit. It works only if you put on the whole suit, not just parts of it. The catalog clearly states, *"Put on the full armor of God"* (Ephesians 6:11).

The Composition of the Power Suit

The Power Suit is made of six parts with two operating instructions.

1. Surround the core of your being with *truth*.
2. Protect your heart with *righteousness*.
3. Wear *peace* on your feet.
4. Wrap yourself in *faith*.
5. Cover your head with *salvation*.
6. Carry the accessory of the *Word of God*.

The operating instructions on the label are twofold. First, *"pray in the Spirit on all occasions with all kinds of prayers and requests."* Second, *"with this in mind, be alert and always keep on praying for all the saints"* (Ephesians 6:18).

One Final Word in Review

I'm sure you've heard of the armor of God before, and you may have even attempted to implement it into your life. But as we look around, we see women struggling to live the moral, godly lives they know they should live. The battle seems too fierce, the war too long, the combat too difficult. We can find ourselves down more than up. Or blindsided and shaking our heads, wondering what hit us. The armor just doesn't seem to be working as it should.

As I mentioned earlier, I contend that our defeats in spiritual battles are not because of any defect in the Power Suit, but because of problems with the fit. Many of us are changing our kind of underwear so that no panty-lines will show, and bra manufacturers are answering our call for smooth bust lines by designing bras with no seams. We'll make these clothing changes in regard to our outer garments without abandoning the bulky spiritual junk that keeps the Power Suit from fitting and protecting us properly. We must remember and understand that the Power Suit of God won't operate unhindered unless we get rid of some old "clothes" first.

This book challenges us as women to get into that dressing room before our Master. Let Him point out to each of us the hindering junk we need to take off and allow Him to tailor the Power Suit to fit our feminine frame.

Chapter 2

Good Foundation Garments

The Belt of Truth

In junior high science class, we learned about human internal organs. For some reason, I was fascinated by the process of the exchange of oxygen and carbon dioxide in the body. The teacher told us that the body's tissues need oxygen to be healthy. She also told us working tissues use up oxygen and produce carbon dioxide that our bodies must release. When we inhale, oxygen enters our lungs and goes into our blood, as carbon dioxide leaves our blood and enters our lungs. When we exhale, we release carbon dioxide because it is poison to our bodies. The teacher impressed on us the importance of keeping our lungs clean by not smoking so that this necessary gaseous exchange could take place freely.

It was even more amazing to discover that I didn't have to worry about reinhaling released carbon dioxide, because plants actually need it to survive. Plants "breathe" carbon dioxide and give off oxygen. (That's why talking to your plants helps them to grow.)

Let's use oxygen as a metaphor for truth—the belt of truth—the first part of the Power Suit. As oxygen is necessary for our physical health, so truth is necessary for our spiritual well-being. It makes sense that a discussion about truth comes first, because truth is the foundation that guides everything that we do.

Just as it is important to protect our lungs that handle our oxygen, it's necessary to protect our gut, which handles truth. Physically, God has placed the rib cage in front of our lungs and other vital organs in order to protect them. Protected and healthy lungs cause us to breathe efficiently, and what we take in and let out needs to be pure or true.

Truth is the rib cage that protects our *spiritual* lives. Everything on which we base our faith must be grounded in truth. If we allow any iota of falsehood to break through, our faith will waver, we'll lose our footing, and the enemy can pierce through our suit with some form of destruction. Hence the admonition in Ephesians 6:14 (KJV), *"Stand therefore, having your loins girt about with truth"*; or *"Stand firm then, with the belt of truth buckled around your waist"* (NIV).

The phrase *"loins girt about with truth"* is packed with powerful meaning. The word *girt* means the "binding on of an item, like a coat or belt, in preparation for something." *Loins* carries with it the idea of our procreative power. When our loins are girt about with truth, we are then prepared to reproduce in others what we have that is sure.

When I was pregnant with each of my sons, I watched closely what I ingested, because I knew everything I took in would affect the baby. In other words, my procreative power would be strengthened or weakened by whatever I took in. I wanted healthy babies, so I consumed healthy food.

Pregnancy and the physical reality of the exchange of gases in the body teach us to do whatever we have to do to protect the process that allows us to take in clean oxygen. In the spiritual realm, we must do whatever we have to do to protect the process that allows us to take in truth. There are several spiritual certainties:

When we breathe in what's good (what's true), we remain healthy.

If we're not careful about what we allow to enter us, we can cause damage to others and ourselves.

When we have truth in us, we're able to give out truth to others. We are not meant to keep every good/true thing for ourselves.

Finally, if we allow that which is not good or that which is untrue to infiltrate our lives, the first piece of the Power Suit won't fit properly, allowing our adversary opportunity to do us harm.

What Gets in the Way of the Fit of the Power Suit Belt?

Let's deal with this final point first. If we allow that which is not good or that which is untrue to infiltrate our lives, the first piece of the Power Suit won't fit properly. What gets in the way of truth?

When it comes to those things we as Christians accept as the truth, it never ceases to amaze what we fall for. We will quote popular talk show hosts, turn to horoscopes or old wives' tales, agree with the tenets of cults and superstitions, and even rest in our own stubbornness, before we'll rely on God's Word for our answers. However, God's Word is clear. Jesus prays to God for us. He asks God to *"sanctify them by the truth; your word is truth"* (John 17:17). We are made pure and holy by one thing and one thing only—God's Word, which is truth. While the talk show hosts may give lots of good, common-sense advice, and many people have survived over the years spouting off old wives' tales and other widely-accepted sayings—unless these principles totally agree with God's Word, they're not the truth. Staking life or making decisions based on TV advice and earthly wisdom lead to disaster.

For example, most of us have heard, "God helps those who help themselves." That saying and that concept is unbiblical. The phrase is not in the Bible, and the concept suggests self-reliance rather than total submission to the God of the universe, which the Bible espouses. Not turning to God's wisdom when we are in a jam will cause poor judgments that can lead to disastrous consequences. *"God is our refuge and strength, a very present help in trouble"* (Psalm 46:1 KJV).

 Step Aside: What do these verses say about God's truth?

Psalm 33:20
Psalm 42:5
Romans 8:26

So, bottom line, what gets in the way of truth? Belief in and acceptance of anything other than truth. Romans 1:19–25, especially verse 21, speaks to the dysfunction caused when we refuse to acknowledge the truth:

Because that, when they knew God, they glorified him not as God, neither were thankful; but became vain in their imaginations, and their foolish heart was darkened (Romans 1:21 KJV).

This verse discusses how we slide into situations where we are not acknowledging God's truth. Reading the whole passage mentioned above, we see that God has placed within us a God-shaped vacuum that only He can fill. *"They knew God."* We are talking here about people who have a history with God, a knowledge and understanding of Him. And that knowledge of Him was placed there by Him.

The first move down the slide away from acknowledging God's truth is to know Him yet not glorify Him for who He is. This occurs when we do not honor God for who He is nor give

Him the credit for what He does. It's very easy to overlook God in a culture that pushes us to glorify ourselves. Mantras like "Take care of number one"; "Watch your back"; and "I deserve it" bombard our thoughts and invade our philosophy. We give evolution the credit for creation, doctors the credit for healing, and the Internet credit for match-making.

Not acknowledging God renders us foolish and destroys our moral judgment (they "became vain"). This then leads to doubtful reasoning and debate ("imaginations") because our thoughts and feelings are unintelligent, wicked, and obscure ("foolish heart...darkened"). In other words, we start accepting craziness as truth. God will allow us to slide away from Him of our own free will when we decide to change the truth of God into a lie.

For example, students are not acknowledging the position of their teacher when they disobey. They are substituting the truth of who the teacher is with a truth they've made up that says they can do whatever they want. Once they decide that's their new truth, they end up suffering the consequences associated with not acknowledging what's really true — the fact that their teacher is in charge. You see, your personal decision about the truth holds no validity unless it is grounded in that which actually is the truth. However, once students acknowledge who is the teacher, that acknowledgement carries with it the idea of adherence to what the teacher says. Consequently, their obedience helps them to reap the benefits of learning what is being taught.

> God will allow us to slide away from Him of our own free will when we decide to change the truth of God into a lie.

In the same way, we fail to acknowledge who God is when we disobey Him. We are acting in accordance to some other truth that says *we* are in charge. Once we begin acting on this new belief, we end up suffering the consequences associated with failing to acknowledge what's actually true — the fact that God is in charge. Acknowledging who God is carries with it the idea of adherence to what He says. Consequently, our obedience leads us to reap the benefits accorded to His children: peace, joy, contentment, and so much more.

 Step Aside: In what way have you been disobeying God, not acknowledging Him as the One in control?

Inhale What's True and Good and Remain Healthy

So now that we understand the foolishness of not accepting God's truth, let's return to the point made earlier that we must do whatever we have to do to be sure we're taking in truth rather than error. The first reality is that spiritual inhalation mirrors physical inhalation; breathing in what's true is as beneficial to us as physically breathing in clean air.

Many people do their best not to breathe in secondhand smoke. Someone else's exhalation of the poisons of a cigarette or cigar pollutes the air others breathe, and many public areas ban smoking for this reason. Do we strive to be as careful about the truth we allow to enter our minds? What each of us believes defines who each of us is and guides what we do.

We can be careful what we "inhale" as truth. The Bible defines truth and tells us of its benefits. Bottom line, God's Word is truth. The Old Testament says it: *"Thou art near, O LORD; and all thy commandments are truth"* (Psalm 119:151 KJV). The New Testament echoes: *"Sanctify them by the truth; your word is truth"* (John 17:17 NIV). John drives home the centrality of the truth when he writes to us, *"In the beginning was the Word…and the Word was God…and the Word was made flesh and dwelt among us"* (John 1: 1, 14 KJV).

The truth is the Word, and the Word is Jesus Himself. However, if we disbelieve the psalmist and don't want to believe John, we must believe Jesus' words. He asserts of Himself, *"I am the way, **the truth**, and the life: no man cometh unto the Father, but by me"* (John 14:6 KJV; emphasis added).

The great news is this: Belief in the truth of God's Word is accompanied by many benefits. The truth is sanctifying, purifying, freeing, and as we are discussing in this chapter, a vital part of the Christian armor that protects our spiritual life.

THE TRUTH IS SANCTIFYING: *"Sanctify them through thy truth: thy word is truth"* (John 17:17 KJV). The truth of God's Word sets us apart for God's special use.

THE TRUTH IS PURIFYING: *"Seeing ye have purified your souls in obeying the truth through the Spirit unto unfeigned love of the brethren, see that ye love one another with a pure heart fervently"* (1 Peter 1:22 KJV). The truth of God's Word cleans us up, allowing us to reach out in love to others just as God would.

> The truth is sanctifying, purifying, freeing, and as we are discussing, a vital part of the Christian armor that protects.

THE TRUTH IS FREEING: *"And ye shall know the truth, and the truth shall make you free"* (John 8:32 KJV). The truth of God's Word is the source of deliverance or liberation from whatever enslaves us.

The liberation of my purified love sets me apart to be used by God in the lives of others. This is the truth that surrounds me, the truth that is holding things together—*"girt about"* our loins—thus, the first part of the Power Suit, and the part that won't fit if we're trying to live by words or philosophies that are not true.

How We Damage Ourselves and Others

The second spiritual reality related to taking in what's good and true is that if we're not careful about what we allow to enter into us, we can cause damage to ourselves and others. Simply put, God's truth is our overall protection. Without it, we will get hurt, and we can hurt others.

The example of smoking cigarettes is again a perfect picture of this point. Those who smoke not only inhale poisons that slowly damage their bodies but also put others around them at risk because of toxins released into the air.

Spiritually speaking, every time we believe that which is not true, we damage ourselves and pass what we believe onto others. If those others, in turn, take in what we've said, we've effectively poisoned their minds and hearts as well.

We see this clearly with the prejudicial ideas and attitudes that run deep in and between people groups—those who differ culturally. Whether we want to admit it or not, many of us hold unfounded stereotypical views about others, based on ignorance and lies. Some people have a superiority complex, stereotyping individuals of different appearance, language, and cultural habits as "lazy," or "ruthless" in financial pursuits, or prone to be "involved in gangs," or "likely to be engaged in organized crime," or "more athletic," or "better in math and science," or "not equal" to some imagined standard.

How ridiculous labels are. And we as Christians should be especially ashamed of ourselves for perpetuating these ideas when Jesus clearly tells us to love our neighbors as ourselves. We hate to be stereotyped; how dare we continue to stereotype others. This is a classic case of accepting something other than the truth, to our detriment, and consequently, the detriment of others with whom we share these thoughts. Stereotypes and myths have no part in the fabric of Christian community, especially as we seek to influence others for Christ.

Accepting prejudicial ideas will hinder us from seeing people as God would have us see them. These views will impede the girdle of truth from fitting properly; if it doesn't fit, we are not protected. And, we will be vulnerable to take in, and adversely affected by, *more* lies. Without God's truth protecting us, any of us can become so turned off to people of other cultures and ideologies, that we become of no use to share the love of God with anyone different from ourselves.

 Step Aside: Do you hold any prejudicial, racist, or bigoted views you believe reject God's truth and displease Him? If so, list them here, and write a prayer beside each one, asking God to forgive you, soften your heart, and give you a heart like His toward that individual or group. If you feel really brave, ask God to give you an opportunity to prove through your actions how your heart has sincerely changed.

<u>My Prejudicial View</u>   <u>My Prayer</u>

Another false philosophy many of us hold that keeps the binder or girdle of truth from fitting us properly is commonly heard in Christian circles in one form or another: God "understands" and winks at sin; *after all, I'm only human.* What an insidious lie. God's estimate of sin was the Cross—that's nothing to wink at. Our human nature is drenched in wickedness. No matter how good we try to be, in and of ourselves, we're a mess. God's Word tells it plainly, *"All of us have become like one who is unclean, and all our righteous acts are like filthy rags; we all shrivel up like a leaf, and like the wind our sins sweep us away"* (Isaiah 64:6).

We Christians are called to live in opposition to our natural inclinations. We are naturally greedy, selfish, and ruthless. What God understands is that we were hopelessly lost to act wickedly, and that's why He sent Jesus. Now our lives are to be a moment-by-moment fight to beat back human nature and allow God's new nature to shine through. In other words, we must live deliberately in the reality of this truth: our natural inclinations are to be swallowed up in righteousness. Allow the belt of truth to move incorrect ideas and beliefs out. This is what it means to live as a new creature in Christ. We do not have the option of ceasing to be new creatures when we get mad, disappointed, or frustrated with the way things are happening in life.

> Allow the belt of truth to move incorrect ideas and beliefs out. This is what it means to live as a new creature in Christ.

You may still ask yourself, *But how am I hurt by believing that God winks at my sin, and how can it hurt others if I believe this?*

Good question. God has the answer.

You are personally hurt by believing this because you are not seeing sin as God sees it. If you don't see your sin as God sees it, you will continue in it and become entrapped by it.

We've probably known someone entangled in some sort of addiction, addictive behavior, or life situation from which she sees no escape. Maybe it's a sister in an abusive marriage, a best friend abusing medication, or an adult daughter suffering through obesity due to emotional eating. Whatever the reason, if that person is a good friend, no doubt it hurts us to see her suffering and struggling in addiction. However, there's basically not much anyone can do for her until she sees the problem for what it really is and decides she's had enough.

You will remain crippled by your sin as long as you refuse to see it for the death-producing evil that it is. Sin always kicks you out of where you ought to be. The ambitious sin found in Lucifer got him kicked out of heaven. The disobedient sin of Adam and Eve got them kicked out of the Garden of Eden. The adulterous sin of David with Bathsheba and his murderous sin in light of it got him kicked out of maintaining peace in his family relationships with his children. And the lying sin of Ananias and Sapphira got them kicked out of this life. Not acknowledging that your sin is what it is will get you kicked out of your blessings. That's how it hurts you to believe that God winks at your sin.

Step Aside: What sin(s) are you now participating in that you have been excusing, feeling "God understands" or "God's winking at this one"? List them and decide on one prayerful and determined step to move you away from the commission of it.

My Sin	My First Step to Move Away from this Sin

By now, it should also be clear how we can hurt others by believing that God overlooks sin. You see, if you believe this to be true, you're likely to pass on this philosophy to your friends, children, co-workers, and others. If you do this, and those people believe you, they will be headed toward the same trouble outlined above. And if you are the one who has caused someone else to stumble and sin, you're in trouble. Take a look at what the Bible has to say about causing others to sin:

Jesus said to His disciples: "Things that cause people to sin are bound to come, but woe to that person through whom they come. It would be better for him to be thrown into the sea with a millstone tied around his neck than for him to cause one of these little ones to sin" (Luke 17:1–2).

Be careful, however, that the exercise of your freedom does not become a stumbling block to the weak. For if anyone with a weak conscience sees you who have this knowledge eating in an idol's temple, won't he be emboldened to eat what has been sacrificed to idols? So this weak brother, for whom Christ died, is destroyed by your knowledge. When you sin against your brothers in this way and wound their weak conscience, you sin against Christ. Therefore, if what I eat causes my brother to fall into sin, I will never eat meat again, so that I will not cause him to fall (1 Corinthians 8:9–13).

Believe it or not, another detrimental false philosophy many Christians accept as true is: All religions lead to the same God. No matter what name is on the marquee, churches that teach the fundamental truths of the Bible, acknowledging first and foremost the deity of Jesus Christ, are leading their parishioners to the God of Christianity. However, any religion not willing to assert that Jesus Christ is God—and the coming to Him in faith for eternal life—is not leading its followers to the same God we serve.

Why in the world would Christians believe, then, that all religions lead to the same God? I can think of three reasons: a misunderstanding of the concept of tolerance, laziness, and misinformation.

Our culture throws around the word *tolerance* like a magic force field designed to deflect any negative comments or criticism. You are labeled intolerant if what you have to say about an individual or a group is disliked by that individual or group, even if your comment is true. The true definition of *tolerance* has to do with respecting the views of others without necessarily sharing those views. While tolerance carries with it the idea of being fair, and even permissive, it is not the same as *acceptance*, which carries with it the idea of approval. Those who knock Christians for standing against such social controversies as gay marriage and abortion rights call them intolerant when, in fact, those believers are simply disapproving such activities based upon the tenets of their faith. So, for example, it's a misunderstanding of the concept to call a Christian intolerant if she can work congenially side by side with a homosexual while not approving of his or her lifestyle. Tolerance and approval are two totally separate issues.

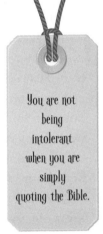

You are not being intolerant when you are simply quoting the Bible.

We don't want to step on anybody's toes. When others speak passionately about their religious beliefs, we feel we'd be seen as intolerant if we assert what the Bible claims. We fold under the intolerance threat and actually begin to believe that the nice people we know of other faiths will get to God their way because they are so sincere.

According to the Bible, although those nice people are sincere, they are sincerely wrong. The plain truth of Scripture is that Jesus clearly identifies Himself as the only way to get to God. (See John 14:6.) My question is: Why is it OK for every other religion to publicly profess its views when it's not OK for Christians to publicly profess theirs? You are not being intolerant when you simply quote the Bible.

Laziness has also moved Christians to believe there is more than one way to get to God. This is an excuse we use for not witnessing, a cover-up for not knowing how to defend the gospel. We'd rather let ourselves be comforted by thinking everybody's OK with whatever god they serve rather than take up the challenge to do some serious apologetics. A former pastor of mine used to say, "Cultists know their error better than we know our truth." How accurate. We lose the battle on the doorstep with the Jehovah's Witnesses every time when we are too lazy to find the Scriptures that prove that Jesus Christ is God.

This laziness shows up as apathy too. By being unable or unwilling to speak up and assert that there is only one way to God — Jesus — we essentially show we're unaware of the reality of hell in the future for everyone we refuse to persuade, and who continues to believe otherwise. We act as though we really just don't care if they go to hell or not.

Finally, some of us are merely misinformed on the issue of how to get to God. Our misinformation concerns what truth is, who God is, and the end results of our belief.

First, we must understand that all truth is narrow. By definition, truth eliminates everything else. Three plus two equals five. That is the statement of a true fact. Five is the only possible correct sum. All other numbers in existence, all other possible answers to that math problem, are eliminated. Well, my goodness. Look how "narrow" that is.

The same is true of the way to get to God. As alluded to earlier, John 14:6 clearly states, *"Jesus answered, 'I am the way and the truth and the life. No one comes to the Father except through me.'"* Here are a few more proof texts:

ACTS 4:12 *"Salvation is found in no one else, for there is no other name under heaven given to men by which we must be saved."*

1 PETER 3:18 *For Christ died for sins once for all, the righteous for the unrighteous, to bring you to God. He was put to death in the body but made alive by the Spirit.*

1 JOHN 2:23 *No one who denies the Son has the Father; whoever acknowledges the Son has the Father also.*

Second, we are misinformed on the issue of how to get to God, because either we don't believe or we don't have a clear understanding of who God is. If we contend that there is only one God, then He is who He is. If all religions lead to God, and there is only one God, He would be the same in every religion.

His attributes would be the same; His requirements would be the same; His words would be the same from faith to faith.

This obviously is not the case. The gods worshipped by different religions around the world manifest themselves in totally different, sometimes completely contradictory, ways. Some gods are reached based upon the amount of work done by the adherent. Some gods are distant and harsh. Some live in inanimate objects.

I am who I am. I have brown skin, I'm five feet five inches tall, and I like chocolate chip cookie dough ice cream. No matter who is talking to me and what name they are using—Sharon, Mom, Honey, or Mrs. Elliott—my attributes do not change. If they did, those people would be talking to a different person, not to me.

It's the same with God. Among other attributes, the Bible teaches He's immutable, omniscient, omnipotent, omnipresent, and jealous when it comes to giving glory to any god. He has revealed Himself to humankind through His Son, Jesus Christ. If religious people are worshipping a god who does not have the same attributes and has not revealed Himself through Jesus, they are not worshipping the same God Christians serve.

Finally, we are misinformed on the issue of how to get to God if we don't see that the end results of various faiths are different. If all roads were to lead to the same God, all of the end results would be the same. Either to be absent from the body is to be present with the Lord (2 Corinthians 5:8), or to be absent from the body is to cease from existence, or is to have another chance to live again. Either it is appointed unto man once to die and after that the judgment (Hebrews 9:27), or we are living by chance with no one running anything and when we die, that's just it. We either face judgment (Revelation 20:12), or our *karma* decides what happens next. You see, we can't have it every way. Again, by definition, absolute truth eliminates every other possibility.

> We are misinformed on the issue of how to get to God if we don't see that the end results of various faiths are different.

Hopefully this clearly explains how each of us can hurt others, and why the belt of truth related to the Power Suit will not fit if any of us believes philosophies that run counter to the truth revealed in the Bible.

Take in Good; Give Out Good

The third spiritual reality related to taking in what's true and good is that we're then able to give out what's true and good for others. What is within can come forth. I can give out an answer only on a subject I've studied or had some contact with in the past. Since I am born in sin, impurity is all I have to offer from my original state. No matter what good I may attempt, at the end of the day, it will count for nothing eternal because it is not rooted in God, who is the ultimate good.

The Bible explains it this way, *"Likewise every good tree bears good fruit, but a bad tree bears bad fruit. A good tree cannot bear bad fruit, and a bad tree cannot bear good fruit"* (Matthew 7:17–18). Also, James 3:11–13 says, *"Can both fresh water and salt water flow from the same spring? My brothers, can a fig tree bear olives, or a grapevine bear figs? Neither can a salt spring produce fresh water. Who is wise and understanding among you? Let him show it by his good life, by deeds done in the humility that comes from wisdom."*

When you take in what's good, you have good available to give out to others. Anything good we have has come to us from God. We came into the inheritance of all He has through His truth.

> *Every good and perfect gift is from above, coming down from the Father of the heavenly lights, who does not change like shifting shadows. He chose to give us birth through the word of truth, that we might be a kind of firstfruits of all he created* (James 1:17–18).

With the Power Suit belt of truth snugly fit around us, we can be God's ambassadors dispensing His truth to others.

God's truth tells me to respect my husband. The King James Version uses the word *reverence*. That includes being there for him when he's in need and extending myself for his comfort. In recent years, my husband, James, suffered a medical emergency. I left work early many days to take him to various doctors' appointments and hospital visits. Once he was home resting, he couldn't do all the things he was used to doing. One thing he appreciates is reading the newspaper every day, which he used to get at work. So while he was recuperating, I would leave the house a little earlier on weekdays, go to the corner convenience store, buy a paper, and bring it back home to him before I went to work. I considered that simple gesture a way to do good and an act of obedience to the truth of God's Word that I should value and respect my husband and his needs.

God's truth tells me to respect my husband.

 Step Aside: What are some good things you can do for others as a response to some truth that has been revealed to you in God's Word?

One Final Thought

An episode of a popular TV show informed women that we quite possibly had been wearing the wrong bra. The studio was transformed into a retail store bra department and the hostess invited her entire audience to test out the theory. Lo and behold, the women discovered that for years they had been wearing the wrong size brassieres; consequently, their breasts weren't being properly supported, and their outer garments weren't hanging on them as beautifully as they should have been. In order to get things right, those women had to take off their old bras, be properly measured, and then put on the new bras right up against their skin with nothing worn underneath. How silly it would have been of them to request to keep wearing their old bra, a T-shirt, or their sweater while the assistants were doing their best to properly fit them with a brand new bra.

How amazingly similar is this revelation to our current discussion. The Power Suit's belt of truth is like the undergarment that must fit properly for our protection and support, and in order for all the other parts of the suit to conform to us beautifully. How silly of me to insist on holding onto old beliefs and philosophies while the Holy Spirit is doing His best to fit me with the truth of God's Word, to enable me to live an abundant life.

The Power Suit belt of truth is designed as the first level of protection from the assault of the devil. When you don't believe the truth of the Word of God, and in turn, believe that which is not true, those falsehoods bulk up under the belt and cause it not to fit. And if that belt doesn't fit, you are unprotected, and your life is vulnerable to the attacks of the enemy. You're flapping around in the wind, exposed to Satan's devices, being injured. Why? You are operating in untruths, either ignorantly or stubbornly, thereby injuring yourself and others.

Each of us must take care not to ingest the poison of what is untrue according to the Word of God. In this way, we will keep our spiritual body healthy. Physically, if something impure does try to get into your body, your healthy system works to purge impurities. Spiritually, when you have truth protecting you, the purging takes the form of discernment, and you are able to ward off the lies seeking to gain a foothold in your life.

Section 2
Righteousness and Peace

Chapter 3

Suited Up

The Breastplate of
Righteousness

Peeople-watching is fascinating: *Where are they going, and where have they been? Are they happy, living the lives they feel meant to live?* Sometimes I'm moved to pray for someone I've just seen in passing; after all, God knows what's going on with that person even though I never may. It's a cool prayer to pray that the person fulfills his or her passion and experiences the desires of his or her heart.

It's important to focus on the heart. Physically speaking, since the hollow, pumplike organ that circulates blood is the workhorse of the body, we really should take better care of it. Sadly, on average, we women don't. According to the National Heart, Lung and Blood Institute Web site, heart disease is the number 1 killer of US women. In fact, 1 in 4 women dies of heart disease. The Web site of the Women's Heart Foundation reported 267,000 of us die each year from heart attacks, which kill 6 times as many women as breast cancer. Another 31,837 women die each year of congestive heart failure, representing 62.6 percent of all heart failure deaths.

In addition to our understanding of the workings of our physical hearts, we also understand our hearts, biblically speaking, to be the center of the total personality, with reference to intuition, feeling, or emotion.

Just as the health of our physical heart directly contributes to the maintenance of a healthy physical life, the health of our spiritual heart determines the vitality of our spiritual life. Just as we should protect our physical heart, God expects us to protect our spiritual heart too. After all, not only is it the heart that has the capacity for sympathy, feeling, and affection, but it's the heart that connects us to God. Sadly, as with the negative physical heart facts above, our spiritual heart-health seems to be in woefully bad shape too.

The Bible has a lot to say about spiritual heart disease. For example:

"For out of the heart come evil thoughts, murder, adultery, sexual immorality, theft, false testimony, slander" (Matthew 15:19).

"The good man brings good things out of the good stored up in his heart, and the evil man brings evil things out of the evil stored up in his heart. For out of the overflow of his heart his mouth speaks" (Luke 6:45).

"He that trusteth in his own heart is a fool: but whoso walketh wisely, he shall be delivered" (Proverbs 28:26 KJV).

You may be thinking: *My goodness, I'm doomed. I may not have it all together, but by and large, I thought I was a woman with a pretty good heart.* Sorry, but Jeremiah 17:9 smacks us right in the vanity and brings those high thoughts of ourselves right down to size. *"The heart is deceitful above all things and beyond cure. Who can understand it?"* The Hebrew word for *deceitful* means "crooked and polluted." In other words, we're a mess.

That's why Proverbs 4:23 warns us, *"Above all else, guard your heart, for it is the wellspring of life."* Isn't that amazing? We need to watch out for our own heart. Since the heart is the source of the mental, emotional, and spiritual appetites, and we actively pursue our appetites, we must find a way to be sure the heart is both protected from its own evil and focused on what's good and right. We not only have to be actively attentive, but we must be real about the deep-seated cravings within our hearts. What we don't pay attention to *will* hurt us. James 1:14 tells us that we are tempted, enticed, and drawn away by our own lusts. Face it: the vast majority of our falls, foibles, and failures are our own fault. Nobody had to help us.

I know, because I had to discover this shocking reality about myself.

After my divorce, I bounced too quickly into a rebound relationship with an ex-boyfriend. (Now there are, no doubt, exceptionally good reasons why an ex-boyfriend *is* an ex-boyfriend, but time and extenuating circumstances play havoc on our common sense and make us forget those reasons. This is a topic for an entirely separate book, isn't it?) He had gotten wind of my troubles and reappeared in my life like the rescuing cavalry. I had been so enamored with this man in the past, that I blindly overlooked

He had gotten wind of my troubles and reappeared in my life like the rescuing cavalry.

the past and many obvious, current danger signs. It wasn't until I slid several months into the relationship, and had wasted a considerable amount of emotional energy, that he slipped up and I discovered that he was married.

The decision to end the relationship right then and there should have been immediate, right? *"Kick him to the curb,"* you say. You're correct, but I'm telling you, it wasn't that easy.

I had probably been like you in my resolve never to get involved with a married man before the previous years of devastation happened to my psyche and wore my resistance down to a nub.

No way would I ever date a married man, I'd muse.

Women who do that have no moral integrity, low self-esteem, and just don't care about anyone but themselves, I'd reason.

Married men know better than to even look my way because I'm better than that, I'd try to convince myself.

Even though I'd been duped, here I was—a Christian author and conference speaker, educator, and mother of two young sons, terribly wrapped up in strong emotional ties with a married man.

The lust of my heart immediately kicked into overdrive.

He showed up when you needed him, it whispered. *His marriage must not be fulfilling to him. He's telling you his marriage is over, and he's working through leaving her. Just give him a little more time. Think about it, he dropped everything in his life to be here for you. The spark between you two never went out over all these years. You don't deserve to be alone. He's here. He's filling the empty spaces.*

An invisible magnetic attraction wouldn't let me out of this man's grip, and I didn't know what to do. Instead of dumping him, I decided to give up on myself and the ministry to women God had launched in me. In the words of the older people in church, I was "a wretch undone." There was no way God could use me now. I figured I would become just another one of the walking wounded, struggling through life the best I knew how, hoping to eat the crumbs from the gracious Master's table every once in a while.

However, a year earlier, I had signed a contract to be the keynote speaker at a big women's conference on the East coast, and that event was drawing near. I don't believe in backing out of my commitments, so I asked God for His mercy. *"Please, God,"* I begged, *"anoint me this one last time. The women at this conference deserve Your best. I realize this will be the last time You use me, and I'm fine with that. Just, please, speak to these ladies through me."*

Thank God for His Spirit living in my life. Even when I was at my weakest, His compassion reached out to me. The messages I communicated at that conference were some of the strongest and most precious I've ever delivered. I could literally feel God's presence and anointing. The night before my last message, another speaker gave a message and afterward invited women to the altar for prayer. She walked over to me, placed her hand on my shoulder, and then looked into my eyes and said, "Oh no. God is not finished with you." Startled, I focused on her kind eyes, and the next thing she said broke me into thankful tears. "God loves you." She then went on to tell me of many wonderful things God still had planned for my life and ministry.

On the strength of that renewed message of God's love and acceptance, despite my failures and weaknesses, I returned home no longer depending on my own strength to extricate myself from my situation. I asked God to do it for me. He silenced the lusts of my heart with the longing for His heart. The more I focused on Him, the more my heart became like His. He led me one step at a time away from that unhealthy relationship and back into fellowship with Him.

> She then went on to tell me of many wonderful things God still had planned for my life and ministry.

The shock of coming face-to-face with the depraved possibilities of my own heart brought me to my knees. That's exactly where God wanted me all along, and that's exactly where He wants you. As hard as it is to look your own heart in the face, that's what's necessary if you ever expect to learn to protect yourself from its lusts.

 Step Aside: Is there some area of weakness in which you feel trapped? Have you succumbed to the lusts of your heart, and now find yourself involved in something unhealthy or ungodly? Are you strongly drawn to either start or continue a certain course of action that is clearly not in line with the Word of God? Pray this prayer on the following page now:

Dear God:
I'm involved in/with _____ *or*
I'm thinking about doing _____ .
I know You are not pleased with this but I don't know how to get
untangled. Please help me. Replace the lusts of my heart with the
desires of Your heart. Show me the practical steps I can take and
then give me the fortitude to take them. I thank You in advance
for deliverance. In Jesus' name, amen.

So Now What?

So, you say to yourself, *I really do want to be a good person. I really*
want my heart to be right. Exactly how do I guard my heart so that I'm
not overtaken by its lusts? I'm glad you asked, because the answer
is in allowing God to fit you with the second piece of the Power
Suit—the breastplate of righteousness.

I've heard it said that the definition of insanity is doing the
same thing repeatedly, yet expecting a different result. If life has
not been working for you, make the radical choice to let God
handle your life. Simply stop doing things your way and start
doing things God's way.

God will initiate your transformation by changing your
heart. Start praying David's prayer from Psalm 51:10. *"Create in*
me a pure heart, O God, and renew a steadfast spirit within me." Prayed
in sincerity, this is a prayer God moves on because it's what He
already wants to do.

> *"I will give you a new heart and put a new spirit in you; I will*
> *remove from you your heart of stone and give you a heart of flesh.*
> *And I will put my Spirit in you and move you to follow my decrees*
> *and be careful to keep my laws"* (Ezekiel 36:26–27).

Once this spiritual transaction has taken place, your physical
actions can kick in. When your heart is oriented in the right
direction, you can begin to operate by its renewed controls. Of
the regenerated heart, the Bible says:

"A wise man's heart guides his mouth, and his lips promote instruction" (Proverbs 16:23).

"The heart of the discerning acquires knowledge; the ears of the wise seek it out" (Proverbs 18:15).

When we acknowledge our inability to defend ourselves from ourselves, God will start showing us the practical stuff we can physically do to start changing our situation. The work now moves to our willingness to empty out unrighteousness and replace it with righteousness, otherwise known as "right living." This right living is the protection our regenerated heart needs.

By wearing the breastplate of righteousness, our heart is protected from the corruption and evil with which it used to be filled. As each of us matures as a follower of Christ, our cravings for the things of the Lord will become more and more evident. This puts us in the place to experience Him in all of His blessings. We start to act in accordance with the wisdom God gives, abandoning foolish behavior. Wisdom speaks: *"I walk in the way of righteousness, along the paths of justice, bestowing wealth on those who love me and making their treasuries full"* (Proverbs 8:20–21).

 Step Aside: Say a prayer of thanksgiving now for the new heart God has given to you. Acknowledge His ability to fill it with His desires. Begin to look forward to the ways you will see the outward changes thanks to your inward, heart change.

What Keeps the Breastplate from Fitting Properly?

Now, if you think you've basically arrived and your problems are solved, you're in for a rude awakening. Your decision to depend on God in this area has placed you squarely in the center of Satan's bull's-eye. He didn't have to bother you much before because the mess in your heart was showing out all on its own. Now you've become a threat to the forces of darkness who want nothing more than to keep your Christian light from shining, giving you victory and drawing others to Christ. Congratulations, you have officially entered spiritual warfare.

Spiritual warfare is no heavy concept. It's the conflict of God versus Satan played out through God's highest creation, humankind. Satan knows his ultimate fate, but on his way to it, his plan is to take as many of us with him as possible. Even when he loses our souls to God's side, he doesn't quit. He then launches an offensive to make our Christian influence as anemic as possible. He does this by throwing hindrances in our paths. In essence, he slyly offers us alternatives—other "outfits" besides the breastplate of righteousness that, if we decide to wear them, will not protect our hearts as we need.

So, what exactly are the hindrances to heart protection that leave our lives vulnerably exposed to the upper cuts and right crosses of sin's consequences? The Five I's found in Galatians 5:19–21 and the Sneaky Six detailed in Ephesians 4:22–32 are the 11 culprits causing all the trouble. Any one or any combination of these 11 deal-breakers will form a bulky layer under the breastplate of the Power Suit that will render it inoperable. As we discuss each one, let's examine our wardrobe to see if the layers exist. If so, be doggedly determined (as my friend Kelsey would say) about peeling them off and laying them aside.

The Five I's

Galatians 5:19–21 details the works of the flesh or representative acts of the sinful nature. In other words, the actions listed will flow from a heart that is not yielded to Christ.

The passage reads:

> *"The acts of the sinful nature are obvious: sexual immorality, impurity and debauchery; idolatry and witchcraft; hatred, discord, jealousy, fits of rage, selfish ambition, dissensions, factions and envy; drunkenness, orgies, and the like. I warn you, as I did before, that those who live like this will not inherit the kingdom of God."*

The categories of problems to watch out for — those which cause the breastplate to fit improperly thus hindering its effectiveness — are the Five I's: immorality, impurity, idolatry, improper attitudes, and indecent behavior.

THE FIRST OF THE FIVE I'S IS SEXUAL IMMORALITY. If you are paying attention at all, it's easy to see that the tendency toward sexual immorality begins early in life these days. Constant exposure to sexual images is everywhere. Try driving down any major roadway and you'll see sex selling everything from cars to soft drinks. Little girls' clothes are miniature copies of grown women's apparel, and many times these outfits are imitations of nightclub attire. No wonder by the teen years our young women have mastered a swish and a switch when they walk, a come-hither giggle, and an STD or two.

In January 2010, the Guttmacher Institute published "Facts on American Teens' Sexual and Reproductive Health." Take in a couple of the shocking facts:

> *Nearly half (46%) of all 15–19-year-olds in the United States have had sex at least once.*

By age 15, only 13% of never-married teens have ever had sex. However, by the time they reach age 19, seven in 10 never-married teens have engaged in sexual intercourse.

Most young people have sex for the first time at about age 17, but they do not marry until their middle or late 20s. This means that young adults are at risk of unwanted pregnancy and sexually transmitted infections (STIs) for nearly a decade.

There were 200,420 abortions among 15–19-year-olds in 2006.

—www.guttmacher.org/pubs/fb_teen_sex.html

However much we might like to blame the current sexual-immorality problems on today's younger generation, I contend that our memories are short. This problem has filtered down from us to our children—today's generation of teens and 20-somethings—thanks in large part to the "free love" movement of the 1960s hippie era and our 1970s overt rebellion against all things orderly. Many of you reading this book were young during these movements, perhaps even as one of their direct results. Whether we were brought up in church or not, during the late 1960s and 1970s, we grew up being indoctrinated by society with messages that encouraged us to explore our sexual freedom in a variety of ways in the name of love. Do you remember these phrases?

"Love makes the world go around."
"Make love, not war."
"Love the one you're with."
"Love means never having to say you're sorry."

Once casual bed-hopping became the norm, the legalization of abortion and the scourge of AIDS quickly followed. Sexual promiscuity spiraled out of control even among churched individuals. Bottom line: we just didn't see sex out-side of marriage as sin any longer.

In light of the above, and many other statistics we could quote on the subject, we come to the issue at hand. God may as well have transported Paul to our century and inspired him to write the Book of Galatians today. His discussion of the actions that flow from the sinful nature lists sexual immorality as the number one problem on the list—specifically, adultery and fornication.

Lest there be any confusion, let's make clear what the Bible means by these words. *Adultery* comes from a Greek word *moi-chos/moicheia* [moy-KAY-uh], meaning one who has unlawful intercourse with the spouse of another. An adulterer is a mar-ried person who has sex with someone who is not his or her spouse. *Fornication*, from the Greek word *porneia* [porr-NAY-uh], means illicit sexual intercourse of any kind. The word also means *harlotry*, a term we may not use much these days, but as women, we certainly understand what it means. Metaphori-cally, fornication is "the association of pagan idolatry with doc-trines of, and professed adherence to, the Christian faith," as defined by *Vine's Expository Dictionary of Biblical Words*. In other words, we are not only fornicators when we engage in illicit sex, but we are also fornicators when we try to combine the warped values of our culture with the holy values of our faith. This is exactly what we are doing when we adopt the oh-God-understands-I-have-needs attitude and use it as an excuse for our promiscuity.

God doesn't tell us to run from much, but in this area His Word is clear. *"Flee fornication"* (1 Corinthians 6:18 KJV). Run from it like an Olympic sprinter.

It seems absurdly obvious, but it must be said: the breast-plate of righteousness will not protect our hearts if we continue our involvement in illicit sexual practices. Face it—there's no excuse for this unrighteousness. It's a breastplate blocker that leaves our hearts vulnerable. We are then headed toward having spiritual heart attacks, and that's exactly where Satan wants us.

If Satan can attack our hearts, he can separate us from God and that can, practically speaking, cause spiritual wreckage. Our eternal security is still intact, but our earthly existence is in shambles.

I hear your heart asking, *"But how do I take off sexual immorality without risking crushing loneliness and becoming a prude?"* First of all, before downing being alone, talk to some women who are in intimate relationship with Jesus Christ and experiencing fulfillment in Him, and then talk to some women who are in unhealthy and abusive relationships. Alone is way better than abused, trust me. Secondly, understand the definition of *prude*. A prude is a person who is overly modest or proper in behavior, dress, or speech, especially in a way that annoys others. If modesty annoys others, that's just proof of how far society has slipped to the dark side.

 Step Aside: What are your honest views concerning fornication? Take this little survey.

1. Is fornication unavoidable in today's society?

2. Is it necessary to have intercourse before marriage to test compatibility?

3. Is it necessary to have intercourse before marriage if you ever plan to land a husband?

4. Is fornication just some old fogey idea that God now winks at?

Now line your answers up with the following Scriptures: Romans 6:12–14; 2 Timothy 2:22; Hebrews 13:4; 1 Peter 2:11; Romans 1:24–27; Colossians 3:5.

If your answers to the survey run counter to the verses above, you have some redressing to do in order for your breastplate to fit and protect your heart. Here are some practical steps to get you started.

For single women:
1. Make up your mind to obey God's Word and trust Him with the results in your relationships. Salvation is God's work; obedience is our responsibility. God will not force us to obey. Sometimes I wish He would because that would be much easier, but it just doesn't work that way.

2. Read the above Scriptures once or twice daily, allowing them to replace the ideas your sinful nature has convinced your mind to embrace. We've been brainwashed with the world's version of untruth, so now we must ask God to reprogram our minds with His truth.

3. Tell the men you date early in the relationship that premarital sex simply is not an option, and tell them why. This will weed out those who do not honor your God or your commitment to Him. This is also an effective measure of heart protection, because if the guy leaves, you haven't formed a strong attachment to him.

4. Date men who are committed to Christ themselves. Talk about sexual issues openly and honestly. Keep your eyes and ears wide open for danger signs, and believe what you see and hear. Challenge concepts and actions that make you uncomfortable.

For married women:
1. Safeguard your marriage by maintaining a healthy sexual relationship with your husband (and having sex as often as is possible for you both).

2. Refuse to entertain sexual or romantic thoughts of other men.

3. Avoid compromising situations. For example, when that ex-boyfriend calls you because he still has your cell phone number, end the conversation quickly and delete his number from your phone's memory. Storing that number provides a temptation to think about and possibly to call to hear his familiar, sympathetic voice the next time you argue with your husband.

4. Discuss with your husband when a man who knows you are married flirts with you or approaches you in a way that makes you feel uncomfortable. I tell my husband about handshakes or cheek kisses from other men that are slightly disconcerting or put me ill at ease.

THE SECOND OF THE FIVE I's IS IMPURITY. Impurity (translated *uncleanness* in the KJV) has to do with both moral and sensual actions. This word is coupled with debauchery (translated *lasciviousness* in the KJV), which means conduct and character that is unbecoming, indecent, and unrestrainedly shameless. This conduct includes the use of filthy words and unchaste movements of the body intended to entice in the lusts of the "flesh," according to the *International Standard Bible Encyclopaedia*.

When I read that definition, my mind registered a phrase I had heard at some time in the past referring to how people in the military are expected to behave. Article 133 of the military code discusses "conduct unbecoming an officer and gentleman." The explanation of the offenses that fit this category is as follows, as written by Rod Powers at about.com:US Military:

Instances of violation of this article include knowingly making a false official statement; dishonorable failure to pay a debt;

cheating on an exam; opening and reading a letter of another without authority; using insulting or defamatory language to another officer in that officer's presence or about that officer to other military persons; being drunk and disorderly in a public place; public association with known prostitutes; committing or attempting to commit a crime involving moral turpitude; and failing without good cause to support the officer's family.

As Christians, we should have standards for our behavior at least as high as those in the military. Impure actions like those listed in the military code will weaken the effectiveness of the Power Suit's breastplate. Look at some of the things on that list. How guilty have we been of dodging debts we know we owe, speaking unfavorably about a boss, or holding a letter that's not ours up to the light?

As with our loose views about sexual immorality, we carry some loose views about moral conduct. Again, we can see in today's young people evidence of how far from God's expectations our society has slipped. Rarely did the high school students I have taught actually see their disobediences as wrong. They would only chide themselves if caught. In other words, the nature of an action is not enough for it to be judged as immoral; therefore, there is no need to question their participation in it. For example, cheating is inherently wrong, but when caught and chastised, they have expressed surprise and come up with all sorts of excuses as to why it was necessary.

Again, the kids got these ideas from us. We cheat on our taxes and excuse ourselves by saying the tax laws are unfair; we bad-mouth authority figures like the police or political figures by evoking our freedom of speech; or over-extend ourselves on our credit cards by redefining wants as needs. And what about the dirty jokes we pass around on the Internet? Come on, ladies,

> Impure actions like those listed in the military code will weaken the effectiveness of the Power Suit's breastplate.

we're wearing that which is impure and lascivious. No wonder the breastplate doesn't fit and our hearts are out there in the open to be crushed.

 Step Aside: If the same standards were applied to you as are applied to a military officer, would you be dishonorably discharged from service to our Lord because your conduct is unbecoming a Christian woman? Check yourself. Look closely. Do you:

1. Knowingly make false statements?
2. Fail to pay your debts?
3. Cheat on exams?
4. Open and read letters of another without authority?
5. Use insulting or defamatory language to or about others?
6. Get drunk and disorderly in public places?
7. Associate with known indecent individuals?
8. Fail without good cause to support your family?
9. Commit or attempt to commit crimes involving moral turpitude?

Moral turpitude includes such crimes as arson, fraud, blackmail, burglary, forgery, bribery, perjury, abandonment, kidnapping, murder, rape, prostitution, sodomy, and conspiracy. So, for example, do you bribe your kids instead of expend the energy to discipline them? Do you fraudulently present yourself as someone you're not? Is the time you spend away from your children absolutely necessary or is it a form of abandonment?

THE THIRD OF THE FIVE I's IS IDOLATRY. We might think of idol worship as a pagan ritual, performed by uneducated, and certainly unenlightened, societies. However, it's mainly the three major Abrahamic religions—Judaism, Christianity, and

POWER SUIT

Islam—that condemn the practice. In religions where such activity is not considered sin, the term *idolatry* either doesn't carry anywhere near as much negative weight, or is totally absent.

In my town, many nail salons are owned by Vietnamese women. I've had nail service at shops where the owners are devout Buddhists. Their religion dictates they honor their god by maintaining a small altar. Sometimes, statues have a prominent place. I'm not condoning their practice; I'm explaining it. Until such time as these lovely women come to know God through faith in Jesus Christ, they will probably continue to worship as they have grown to believe. And until we build friendly relationships with them that would invite open dialogue, we can pray that Christian Vietnamese operators in the shop, who speak their language and are their close friends, can find an opening to witness to them.

The absence of the word *idolatry* from a religion's understanding doesn't make the practice OK. If you are driving in another state and break a driving law you didn't know, you'll get a ticket. Your ignorance of the law did not affect the legality of the offense. An entire segment of the Book of Romans is dedicated to the explanation of the fact that before the Law of God was written down, sin still existed, but we simply didn't know it. The Law didn't define sin; it simply pointed it out.

So that is what we are doing here: pointing out the fact that idolatry is the worship of any cult image, idea, or object, as opposed to the worship of God. We may pat ourselves on the back about knowing better than to worship an actual statue of someone or something, but many times we allow other objects or ideas to become such a focus of our attention that they are elevated to idol status.

It's so incredibly easy to become an idol worshipper, it's scary. The line between healthy dedication and unhealthy idolatry can

The absence of the word idolatry from a religion's understanding doesn't make the practice OK.

be rather slim. Without even realizing it, we can slip into idol-
izing our education, job, home, possessions, husband, children,
celebrities, and money. Speaking to writers, my friend Sharon
Ewell Foster put it this way in her newsletter post:

> *When we put contracts, relationships, and best-seller lists ahead*
> *of doing the right thing, then those things are idols in our lives.*
> *Part of our love, part of our ambassadorship means that we must*
> *give up our own thoughts, our own ways, and take on the ways of*
> *Christ. Loving Him first may mean that we have to turn down*
> *some contracts, refuse some authors, or give up some checks for*
> *the sake of the Cross, or that we won't be invited to some parties*
> *or events.*

Notice, too, that the point of idolatry is coupled with witchcraft.
Again, you may be thinking that this is something relegated to
heathen societies, but the Greek word for witchcraft is *pharmak-
eia* [far-mah-KAY-uh] from which we get our word *pharmacy*,
dealing with medication. Witchcraft, then, deals not only with
sorcery, but with drug abuse. Dependence on drugs such as
heroine, cocaine, marijuana, alcohol, nicotine, and caffeine can
move these substances into the area of idol worship as we look
to them to fill needs only God can fill.

God is so serious about our avoidance of idolatry that He
placed His Word about it at the very top of the list of the Ten
Commandments.

> *"I am the LORD your God, who brought you out of Egypt, out*
> *of the land of slavery. You shall have no other gods before me.*
> *You shall not make for yourself an idol in the form of anything*
> *in heaven above or on the earth beneath or in the waters below"*
> (Exodus 20:2–4).

Participation in any form of idolatry creates a bulky layer we
try to wear under the breastplate of righteousness, but idolatry
is unrighteous. We can tell that we have elevated something to

idol status by our reaction if that thing is removed from our lives. Although we naturally feel sorrow about losing something or someone precious, even those losses shouldn't devastate lives that are sincerely dependent upon God. This may sound rather harsh, but if God is who He says He is, He can be trusted to be our Rock when all else around us falls, disappears, or dies. Anything or anyone other than God receiving our worship has become an idol and must be peeled off and relegated to the proper place behind God. Some idols, such as the use of illegal and harmful substances, must be eliminated totally. Some idols—money, the job, the husband, and the children—cannot be removed, but are to be subordinated to God.

We can tell that we have elevated something to idol status by our reaction if that thing is removed from our lives.

 Step Aside: What are your idols? Using earthly people or things, complete the following statement with as many answers as apply: I simply could not go on without...

Whatever you answered may have become an idol to you. Pray about whether that idol can be eliminated, or how you can subordinate it to God. God says He is a jealous God, meaning He refuses to take second place in your life. God has exclusive right to your devotion based upon who He is and what He's done.

THE FOURTH OF THE FIVE I'S IS A CATEGORY WE WILL CALL IMPROPER ATTITUDES AND ACTIONS TOWARD OTHERS. These temperamental sins, as *Wycliffe's Bible Commentary* calls them, are hatred, variance (discord), emulations (jealousy), wrath (fits of rage), strife (selfish ambition), seditions (dissensions), heresies (factions/cliques), envyings, and murders.

The items in this list actually play off of each other. Hatred, an inner or latent reason for opposition, can overflow into variance, which is a contentious quarrel. Nurturing the negativity stirred up by the quarrel fuels emulation, which is heat or zeal. Next comes wrath, a deepening indignation that causes the move to strife, the stage at which we bring others into our negative attitude against another person. We progress from strife to sedition, the stage at which we solidify the disunion we're anxious to seal. After sedition comes heresy, at which level we draw party lines, pulling others to our dark side by making sure both we and they know who's on whose side. Heresy moves to actual envying, at which time we wish ill will upon our enemy.

This whole ugly downward spiral erupts into . . . the murder that manifests as the slaughter of someone's character.

This whole ugly downward spiral erupts into murder, sometimes of physical life, but more often, the murder manifests as the slaughter of someone's character.

How does this look in actual practice? Let's say Almira is a longtime, active member of her church. When Irene, a younger and newer member of the congregation, is appointed as women's ministry director, Almira is placed on her staff. Irene is excited and enters her job as an optimist with all sorts of new and innovative ideas. Almira knows from experience, however, that the women of the church are very slow to adapt and would be won over by being led gradually into the good changes Irene is proposing. Since Irene is already feeling slightly inadequate knowing about the older women's experiences, when Almira suggests moving at a slower pace, Irene silently takes offense. The start of the trouble ensues and inner hatred is fueled.

Irene seethes through every meeting and begins to snap back (variance) every time Almira even slightly disagrees with an idea. These little quarrels become emulation as the heat of the dissent digs in. Irene takes her issue to the next level, strife, when she shares with her best friend, Shelly, her negative feelings toward Almira. Of course, Irene's explanation makes Almira out to be the Wicked Witch of the West, "After whom she must have been named," Irene is quick to point out.

Irene's vitiating comments about Almira continue and Shelly, who had always respected the older woman, begins to interpret Almira's words and actions in the light of Irene's outlook (sedition). Heresy takes hold when Almira misses a women's meeting after which Irene holds a little pity-me powwow with a few of the other younger women. Irene's tearful prayer requests are masking the real outcome she hopes this meeting achieves and that's to draw solid lines of who's on whose side. Once accomplished, Irene actually feels justified having others around now who from their warped perspective "see what Almira is really like." Irene begins to wish ill will upon Almira (envying), rationalizing that Almira needs to be judged to learn a lesson. She takes her complaints all the way to the pastor and does her best to assassinate Almira's character.

Hopefully within our sphere of influence, we surround ourselves with women whose cooler heads can prevail. None of us can grow stronger and wiser surrounded by others who are exactly like us. All of us have weaknesses and can find ourselves sinking into the depths of these improper attitudes and actions. If we find ourselves wearing any one of the attitudes above, it will poke out awkwardly from under the breastplate of righteousness we're trying to wear.

So how do we guard against the fourth of the Five I's? We start by being aware of the improper-attitude cycle and call it what it is—sin. Hatred, variance, emulation, strife, sedition, heresy, envying, murder: each one leads to the next, and each one can be successively more evil. Then as we have been doing with each point in this book, we must be brutally honest with ourselves. Take a hard look at the difficult relationships in your life. See if you find your attitudes anywhere in this list. The deeper into the cycle you are, and the longer you've been in the relationship, the more determined you must be to shake the feelings. Of course, the hardest issues will be those involving family members, so we must be aware of that too.

Each of us must determine to honor God in every one of our dealings with others, which will allow us to embark on our individual journey of peeling off these layers that are causing the breastplate to fit improperly, therefore leaving the heart vulnerable to repeated attack. Do not be ashamed or afraid to seek professional Christian help if necessary to unpack some deep-seated relational issues you cannot get at on your own.

 Step Aside: Ask yourself the following questions in regard to the list of improper attitudes and actions.

HATRED: Do I sense an inner or latent reason to be in opposition to someone?

VARIANCE: Am I prone to start quarrels or pick little fights with anyone in particular?

EMULATION: Do I feel an inordinate burning jealousy against a person?

WRATH: Do I sense a deepening indignation toward someone?

STRIFE: Do I find myself bringing others into my negative attitude against another person?

SEDITION: Am I anxiously trying to solidify the disunion regarding someone?

HERESY: Am I eager to get others on my side against someone in particular?

ENVYING: Do I wish anyone ill will?

MURDER: Am I bent on destroying someone?

THE FIFTH OF THE FIVE I'S THAT KEEPS OUR BREASTPLATE FROM FITTING PROPERLY IS INDECENT BEHAVIOR. In Matthew Henry's well-respected commentary on the Bible, drunkenness, revelings, and the like are considered sins against ourselves.

Although intoxicated people sometimes seem extremely happy and carefree, that's about the extent of the positive points of drunkenness. The *International Standard Bible Encyclopedia*'s electronic database says it negatively causes "forgetfulness, loss of understanding, and balance of judgment." It makes "one oblivious of [her] misery; but it ultimately leads to woe and sorrow and to poverty. . . . Its moral and spiritual effects: . . . lead to a maladministration of justice; provokes anger and a contentious, brawling spirit; and conduces to a profligate life. . . . Above all, it deadens the spiritual sensibilities, produces a callous indifference to religious influences, and destroys all serious thought. . . . While total abstinence [from alcohol] is not prescribed as a formal and universal rule, broad principles are laid down, especially in the New Testament, which point in that direction."

Alcohol overindulgence has been the ruin of many a career, relationship, family, and reputation. We may be free to drink alcoholic beverages as long as we don't get drunk, but we're also free to eat lots of salty, fatty foods. Neither of these freedoms makes the indulgences good for us. Also, we have to think about how our freedom will affect others.

I am very mindful about how my public actions could affect my character and thus my testimony. While attending a wedding reception of a former student, I sat at a table with three of my other former students. These young people are now 20-somethings—official adults. Dennis decided to get an alcoholic beverage from the open bar. When he brought it back to the table, I asked him what he was drinking. He told me some name I'd never heard, and then said, "Oh, you wouldn't really be interested because you don't drink, do you?"

"Every now and then," I admitted, "I have a glass of wine with dinner when my husband and I go someplace special."

When he heard my response, his expression was a hilarious mixture of surprise, wonder, disbelief, and shock. I had only ever functioned in his mind as his English and religion teacher, who would lead chapels with fun-yet-convicting messages about which we'd have long discussions regarding how to make the points practical in a young man's life. To him, alcohol consumption, no matter how slight, just didn't figure into that picture.

Dennis implored me to take a sip of the drink he hadn't yet tasted, just so he could say he had seen the impossible happen once in his life. How funny!

What's my point? Alcohol carries with it such a negative reputation that its very presence in our experience could cause others to question our testimony, or worse yet, could cause others to think imbibing is all right for them since they see us do it. A habit of drunkenness bulks up under our breastplate.

As far as revelings are concerned, let's start by defining the term. The Greek word *komos* may involve letting loose and rioting. Again, the *International Standard Bible Encyclopaedia* says, "The obvious meaning of the word is excessive and boisterous intemperance and lustful indulgence."

This is not saying we Christians cannot have fun. We can and we must reconcile ourselves to the fact that we are expected to live our entire lives within the protective boundaries God has supplied. Basically, it's a bad idea to throw caution to the wind. That saying, and others like it, came to be clichés because of the truth and wisdom they carry.

> Don't go overboard.
> Look before you leap.
> Don't go off the deep end.

Consider police officers. Whether they are home, or at worship, or at the church picnic, they are still police officers. They are trained to be acutely aware of their surroundings 24 hours a day. Even if they are engrossed in a competitive basketball game or an interesting conversation, an odd movement or noise off to the side will capture their attention, and they'll make an immediate evaluation of the situation, seeing if there's a threat involved.

In the same way, we are Christians all the time. Our holiness satellite should always be tuned to the Master's signal. We must be ever acutely aware of keeping our actions within His boundaries. Basically, uncontrolled wildness and craziness is not becoming of a Christian and must be peeled off, as it were, if we expect the breastplate of righteousness to fit properly and offer us the heart protection we need.

Finally, exactly what did God mean by adding the words *"and such like"* (KJV) or *"and things like these"* (NASB) at the end of this Galatians 5 passage? I love how God makes sure to shut us up. He knows our tendency to try to find the loophole. After listing all these sins of the flesh, He negates the possibility of our coming up with something evil we consider to be excusable because it's not on the list. So at the end of God's list, He inserts an et cetera to cover any new twisted sin our depraved nature could invent.

We are Christians all the time. Our holiness satellite should always be tuned to the Master's signal.

The obvious point on drunkenness is: don't drink to excess. Concerning revelings and the like, the point is: don't get carried away, getting involved with evil.

 Step Aside: On drunkenness: Do you drink to excess? What are you going to do to stop that habit? If you drink alcohol at all, would you feel comfortable drinking the way you do if Jesus were physically present with you at the time?

On revelings: Can you think of times when you have lost control of yourself at a party or some other social gathering? Were you proud of yourself? Would God have been pleased with your performance? What precautions can you put into place to be sure something like that does not happen again?

The Sneaky Six

In addition to the bulkiness the Five I's create under your breastplate, don't let the Sneaky Six creep in either. I call these issues sneaky because sometimes we fall into them and don't even realize it. God enumerates them for us. In brief, we see them here in portions of this passage:

> *You were taught, with regard to your former way of life, to put off your old self, which is being corrupted by its deceitful desires; to be made new in the attitude of your minds...put off falsehood and speak truthfully..."In your anger do not sin"...He who has been stealing must steal no longer, but must work...Do not let any unwholesome talk come out of your mouths, but only what is helpful...Get rid of all bitterness, rage and anger, brawling and slander, along with every form of malice. Be kind and compassionate to one another* (Ephesians 4:22–32).

Just in case you missed the list, the Sneaky Six are lying, anger, wrath, bitterness, stealing, and corrupt communication. We already know these issues are problematic, so let's at least mention them in brief to be sure to put us on the lookout, lest they endeavor to cloak themselves and either remain or become a hindrance to our properly fitted breastplate.

First, let's discuss lying.

"How much money did you make last year?" asks the tax preparer.

"Sheila's on the phone, Mom. Do you want to talk to her? What should I tell her?" your daughter asks about the woman from work you are trying to avoid.

"Are you flossing daily?" probes the dentist at your long-overdue appointment.

"Do you know how fast you were driving?" inquires the highway patrol officer from behind the clipboard holding the speeding ticket he is about to write.

"How old are you?"

We are faced almost daily with opportunities to lie or tell the truth. We lie for different reasons, including: to save face because we are embarrassed, to stay out of trouble, to remain in someone's good graces, or just because we're too scared to face up to the consequences of telling the truth. None of these reasons are excused in Scripture.

Apart from something serious like saving a life or something totally benign like pulling off a surprise party, very few reasons exist permitting us to lie. Our key Scripture verse says, *"Put off falsehood and speak truthfully"* (Ephesians 4:25). The Greek word for falsehood is *pseudos* [PSOO-dahss]. This is a familiar prefix we commonly use meaning false, spurious, pretended, or sham. A *pseudonym*, for example, is a fictitious name sometimes used by an author.

A lie is something said, done, or implied with the intent to deceive. A lie can also be something not said. In other words, if our silence causes someone to believe something that is not true, we have lied.

Christians must hate lying (Proverbs 13:5), avoid it (Zephaniah 3:13), pray to be delivered from it (Psalm 119:29), and reject the company of liars, knowing that they will not stand in God's presence (Psalm 101:7), states in the *International Standard Bible Encyclopaedia*. Very harsh punishment is promised to liars.

Liars cannot offer acceptable worship to God (Psalm 24:3–4), and their end is exclusion from heaven (Revelation 21:27; 22:14–15).

Even though this is a women's book, if you are a liar, the most accurate admonition is, "man up." Perhaps we should consider the discontinuance of whatever actions we are involved in that cause us to lie. If we have nothing to hide, we'll have no occasion to lie in the first place. And, as independent adults, apart from representatives of the legal profession, we can choose to whom we reveal certain things. It might help us to learn to respond with, "I'd rather not say" or "That's none of your business" rather than to tell a lie.

Step Aside: If you are having trouble with lying, start today and take one month concentrating on telling the truth no matter what. With a two-column list, chart every instance in which you are tempted to lie. Beside each entry, write down how you were able to face the challenge and tell the truth.

Numbers two, three, and four of the Sneaky Six — anger, wrath, and bitterness — play off of each other. Anger has to do with exasperation, reaching one's wit's end over a personal offense. Wrath, which comes from a Greek word *thumas* [thew-MAHSS] means passion or fierceness as if breathing hard. Settled wrath kicks in when our exasperation reaches a boiling point and turns to actions. These rash actions are inexcusable, because they are self-centered efforts to vindicate oneself. Bitterness is the result of letting anger and wrath settle in. Bitterness (*pikria* [pih-KREE-uh] in Greek) means acridity, especially poison, and is used metaphorically of a condition of extreme wickedness. Bitterness spawns resentment, grudges, feuds, separations, and general bad blood. When the three of these Sneaky Six — anger, wrath, and bitterness — are allowed to run their course together, tragedy is always the result.

Remember the classic Shakespeare tragedy *Romeo and Juliet*? We never concern ourselves with the initial spark of anger between the two men instigating the original conflict, Lord Capulet and Lord Montague, who started the two families feuding in the first place. Whatever the problem, it had never been resolved and had been allowed to grow into wrath. Each side tried to get the other side back over the years, and when we enter the streets of Verona in the opening of the play, the poison of bitterness had firmly drawn the party lines, and the long-standing feud was firmly entrenched. No amount of sensible talk helped. In the end, the families decided to end the feud, but at a cost of a body count of five young people, including the two main, star-crossed lovers.

We allow the anger-wrath-bitterness trio to work its ruin all too often. Jewel* spent her own money to participate in my wedding. She bought her fabric, had her dress made, and bought her airline ticket to fly from the East to the West Coast for the ceremony. A year and a half later, I was unable to attend her wedding because I had just given birth to Matthew, my first son. In the frantic first months of his life, every-thing else paled in comparison to his care, and although I had bought the fabric for the deco-rative pillow I planned to give Jewel as a gift, I never got around to finishing the embroidery on it. In the meantime, Jewel got angry. Her wrath exploded through her phone call as she told me off for my insensitivity and ungrateful-ness. I knew bitterness had taken root because even after I apologized profusely, she held the grudge, and our friendship ended when she refused to have anything to do with me ever again. *Symbol indicates this is not person's real name.

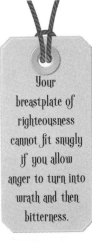

Your breastplate of righteousness cannot fit snugly if you allow anger to turn into wrath and then bitterness.

Anger is a human emotion, but it is controllable. Your breastplate of righteousness cannot fit snugly if you allow anger to turn into wrath and then hold on to bitterness. That's an ugly robe to try to wear under your armor.

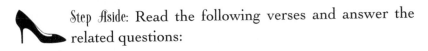

Step Aside: Read the following verses and answer the related questions:

What was the outcome of anger in the situations described in these stories? Genesis 4:5–8; 49:5–8

What do the following verses teach you about anger? Proverbs 19:19; 22:24–25; 25:28; 29:22

If you need some specific areas of anger to look into, are you guilty of any of these New Testament prohibitions on anger? Do you:

1. Allow your anger to vent all over people? (Romans 12:19)

2. Go to bed or let lots of time pass while remaining angry at people? (Ephesians 4:26)

3. Remain angry with people rather than seek reconciliation? (Matthew 5:22–26)

4. Communicate an angry spirit when involved in the training and upbringing of your family? (Colossians 3:19; Ephesians 6:4)

If you answered yes to any of the above, do some anger management and determine to operate more civilly. You may need to enlist the help of a faithful friend who is not afraid of your outbursts and to whom you will listen when she sees your anger rising to inappropriate levels.

"Stolen water is sweet; food eaten in secret is delicious!" (Proverbs 9:17). Since the beginning of time, literally, we've been sucked in by things we're not supposed to have. Eve had to have some of that fruit. Adam couldn't resist either. We not only crave what we can't have, but we seem to like its acquisition better. But as with Adam and Eve, things stolen are poison. There are always disastrous strings attached. Taking that which is not ours to take—stealing—is number five of the Sneaky Six sins that bunch up under the breastplate, keeping it from fitting properly.

Let's explore some examples of stealing that we may not think of very often. We're stealing when:

We fiddle around with our time at work. (In other words, we say we arrived earlier than we actually did, or we leave early, unbeknownst to our employer.)

We tap into someone else's cable line.

We duplicate copyrighted CDs and DVDs. (When we do this, we are stealing income from the artist or actor. The Berne Convention for the Protection of Literary and Artistic Works has protected the copyrights on literary, scientific, and artistic works since 1886. Article 9 of the Convention states that: *Authors of literary and artistic works protected by this Convention shall have the exclusive right of authorizing the reproduction of these works, in any manner or form. . . . Any sound or visual recording shall be considered as a reproduction for the purposes of this Convention* Simply stated, only the creator of the work has the right duplicate it. If that creator hasn't duplicated it, we have to buy it if we want it for ourselves.

We buy bootleg CDs and DVDs. (When we buy bootlegged and pirated discs, we are both financing crime and stealing from the artist.)

We plagiarize—taking someone else's words or ideas and presenting them as if they were our own. (Plagiarism includes not only school term papers, but also taking the credit at work for someone else's idea, or copying an outline of a speech someone else delivered, and then speaking it as if it were our idea.)

We pay less tax than we rightfully owe. (I'm not talking about legal deductions. We are stealing from the government when we lie on our tax returns in order to avoid paying what the law says we owe. The main way to pay less tax is to make less money. Is that what you want?)

We lie to gain additional scholarship money for our children. (If our child gets money to which he or she is not honestly entitled, we are stealing from someone else's child who might not get a college education at all without it.)

We deliberately outshine someone else's proud moment. (This point sounds like this, "Well, you may have done x, y, or z, but I...")

When it comes to stealing, God simply says, "Stop it." Ephesians 4:28 is not one of those verses for which we need a seminarian's interpretation. *"He who has been stealing must steal no longer, but must work, doing something useful with his own hands, that he may have something to share with those in need."* We buy pirated DVDs because we either cannot or don't want to pay full price. This verse is telling us plainly to work so we'll earn the money to legally purchase what we want and need. Then, when we've earned our money, we should think about how we can help others in need rather than try to cheat our way through.

THE SIXTH OF THE SNEAKY SIX IS CORRUPT COMMUNICATION OR UNWHOLESOME TALK. This phrase means speech that defiles; speech that is rotten, worthless, of poor quality, and unfit for use. Instead of speaking in this way, our current passage (Ephesians 4) quickly tells us to speak only that which is *"helpful for building others up according to their needs, that it may benefit those who listen"* (v. 29).

Have you ever known someone who just always seemed to find the good in everybody and in every situation? I met a woman like that when I was speaking at a conference once. We became fast friends and that's the first thing I noticed about her. Chaundra could find the positive side in every situation we discussed. Even when she shared times that were difficult in her personal life, her ending remarks would be redeeming.

Cursing, talking down, discouraging, gossiping, and name-calling are all examples of communication that can be labeled as corrupt. We are not building people up when we label them negatively, curse at them, or are quick to point out what they cannot achieve. This sort of talk fits under the Sneaky Six heading because the tendency to talk this way can do that—sneak up on us. Who can be guilty of corrupt communication?

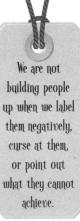

We are not building people up when we label them negatively, curse at them, or point out what they cannot achieve.

A frustrated single mom who, after fighting with her ex-husband over child support, faces disciplining her son about bad grades for the fifth time this month. She blurts out, "You are headed for being no good, just like your father."

Discouraged co-workers who, after being passed up for the third time for the promotion they feel they deserve, chide the new supervisor by saying, "Only kiss-ups are placed in your position because management chooses who they can control."

Embittered church members who find it necessary to snuff out the eagerness of a newer member by submitting gossip veiled as a prayer request that says, "Pray for Evelyn whose overzealous spirit is clearly a ploy for more attention from the pastor."

The Bible warns us about the terrible nature and misuse of our tongue and words.

Why do you boast of evil, you mighty man? Why do you boast all day long, you who are a disgrace in the eyes of God? Your tongue plots destruction; it is like a sharpened razor, you who practice deceit. You love evil rather than good, falsehood rather than speaking the truth. Selah. You love every harmful word, O you deceitful tongue! (Psalm 52:1–4).

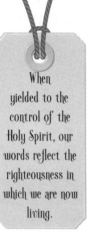

When yielded to the control of the Holy Spirit, our words reflect the righteousness in which we are now living.

"Likewise the tongue is a small part of the body, but it makes great boasts. Consider what a great forest is set on fire by a small spark. The tongue also is a fire, a world of evil among the parts of the body. It corrupts the whole person, sets the whole course of his life on fire, and is itself set on fire by hell. All kinds of animals, birds, reptiles and creatures of the sea are being tamed and have been tamed by man, but no man can tame the tongue. It is a restless evil, full of deadly poison. With the tongue we praise our Lord and Father, and with it we curse men, who have been made in God's likeness. Out of the same mouth come praise and cursing. My brothers, this should not be" (James 3:5–10).

The corrupt use of our tongue and words must be stopped before our breastplate of righteousness will fit and properly protect our hearts from the onslaughts of our enemy. The great news is that even our tongues can be redeemed. When yielded to the control of the Holy Spirit, our words will reflect the righteousness in which we are now living. Look at some of the positive things the Bible has to say about the tongue and the lives of those who submit theirs to His control:

Proverbs 10:20 *The tongue of the righteous is choice silver.*

Proverbs 10:31 *The mouth of the righteous brings forth wisdom.*

Proverbs 10:32 *The lips of the righteous know what is fitting.*

Proverbs 25:15 *Through patience a ruler can be persuaded, and a gentle tongue can break a bone.*

Psalm 15:1–3 *LORD, who may dwell in your sanctuary? Who may live on your holy hill? He whose walk is blameless and who does what is righteous, who speaks the truth from his heart and has no slander on his tongue, who does his neighbor no wrong and casts no slur on his fellowman.*

Step Aside: How much of your speech can be considered helpful or edifying? For the next 30 days, experiment with finding something positive to say about every situation that upsets you. Be sincere. Don't deny your frustration or hurt, but find at least one silver lining to speak about in each cloud. For example, if I have cross words with my husband, I could say, "Well, honey, we may disagree, but I'm glad I have a husband to disagree with." Keep a journal. At the end of the 30 days, evaluate your month of edifying rather than corrupt speech. I bet God will have been pleased with the words of your mouth. You'll probably feel much better too, and you will have saved some relationship headaches along the way.

In Conclusion

At the writing of this chapter, there are wars raging still. The Bible plainly tells us that there will always be actual *"wars and rumors of wars"* (Mark 13:7). It's as true that the war for the ruin of your life will be waged until you die. This chapter has sought not only to convince you of the necessity of protecting your spiritual heart while in combat, but to give you very practical, how-to steps in accomplishing that task. The bottom line is: protect your heart by living righteously.

"In righteousness you will be established: Tyranny will be far from you; you will have nothing to fear. Terror will be far removed; it will not come near you" (Isaiah 54:14). Righteousness establishes who you are as a child of God. You have no reason to live righteously other than the fact that you're doing it because you want to obey God. Many times, righteousness is not fun. In fact, unrighteousness was so much fun, some of us have to try very hard daily to stay away from it. Unrighteousness just fits so well. We are/were so comfortable with it that now that we have become Christians, it's hard for some of us to take it off.

Righteousness is like a form-fitting garment and unrighteousness is like a shift or muumuu.

Righteousness is like a form-fitting garment and unrighteousness is like a shift or muumuu. When you first put on something formfitting, you're conscious about how you look. If you're dieting, a form-fitting outfit shows off all the imperfections you are trying to diminish. However, as you keep working out, unsightly bulges get smaller. Eventually, sleek curves and beautifully formed muscle appear. Now you're excited to wear that form-fitting outfit, and you can't believe you were seen in public in that muumuu.

So it is with righteousness and unrighteousness. At first, righteousness is not comfortable. There is lots of flabbiness—all the stuff we just talked about that makes the breastplate not fit quite properly—and you will continue to feel awkward while you are shedding the weight of unrighteous living. You just won't feel comfortable trying to wear righteousness while you go where you used to go, do what you used to do, talk like you used to talk, and hang around who you used to hang around.

Oh, but if you keep that form-fitting breastplate of righteousness on and keep "working out" the old stuff, you'll find that righteousness fits more and more comfortably on the new you every day. You'll begin to notice that the breastplate of righteousness fits your new spiritual body.

One Final P.S.

As a righteous woman, you will be attacked, so don't be surprised. Satan, your enemy, works diligently to fashion weapons specifically to fit you. (See Isaiah 54:15–17.) The weapon of jealousy he may form for someone else, he couldn't use on you because it wouldn't faze you. But the weapon of lying that he formed just for you could take you right out, while not affecting another person in the least. God's promise, as relates to righteousness, is that as you live right, even the weapons fashioned specifically to take you out won't even be able to hurt you. The blows will hit the breastplate and bounce right off, because the center of who you are is mightily protected.

Chapter 4

Shoes to Match

Feet Shod with the Preparation of the Gospel of Peace

Beautiful shoes are hard for me to resist. The two reasons why I'm not as obsessed about shoes as was Imelda Marcos are my husband and my bank account. Neither James nor my wallet allows me to go overboard purchasing lovely footwear. In my defense, however, I contend that my present love of shoes and attention to my feet were inbred early in life when I was born with clubbed feet. I was so positioned in my mother's womb that I emerged with both feet pigeon-toed and tilted at the ankles. The doctors told my mom I'd walk with difficulty and wear expensive, corrective shoes all my life, or she could place my feet in special baby-shoe braces to fix them while I was still an infant. Mom opted for the latter.

Not long after being brought home from the hospital, I was fitted for special little shoes connected together with a steel bar. The apparatus straightened my feet by repositioning the shoes at new angles every so often until my feet were properly aligned with my ankles and legs. The correction worked. My feet were straight long before I began to stand and walk, and today my gait is perfect. Still, as a newborn, I must have registered two of the doctor's words in my long-term memory—*expensive* and *shoes*— so how could I not love gorgeous footwear today?

I'm at peace with my love of shoes and my level of control when passing through a shoe department. I buy shoes when I need them and can afford them. Both my husband and my wallet are cool with that. However, when we believers are not at peace in our Christian walk, nothing else in life lines up as it should.

But how, you may be wondering, *do you get this point about peace from a comparison being made with shoes?*

Actually, the comparison wasn't my idea: it's in the Ephesians text, and *Matthew Henry's Commentary* explains:

> *Shoes, or greaves of brass, or the like, were formerly part of the military armor. The use of them was to defend the feet against the gall-traps, and sharp sticks, which were laid in the way to obstruct the marching of the enemy, those who fell upon them being unfit to march. The preparation of the gospel of peace signifies a prepared and resolved frame of heart, to adhere to the gospel and abide by it, which will enable us to walk with a steady pace in the way of religion, notwithstanding the difficulties and dangers that may be in it.*

The commentary goes on to explain that being peaceable preserves us from temptations and persecutions in much the same way as the shoes of brass protected the feet and legs of the Roman soldiers. Those warriors couldn't wear strappy sandals, high heels, or flip-flops into battle. Those simply would have been the wrong kinds of shoes for the situation. They would have fallen victim to any trap laid before them. They would have been nervous about every step, and their progress would have been significantly hampered. The wrong kinds of shoes would have caused them anxiety. Only a soldier adequately attired can enter into battle at peace, alert to the onslaughts yet protected from them.

POWER SUIT

We do not live peaceable lives because we're stepping into situations without proper protection and that causes us anxiety. The right kinds of shoes allow us to walk confidently in every particular circumstance in which we find ourselves. Cleats give running backs the ability to have sure footing as they dodge tackles and fight their way to the goal line in football. Extremely lightweight running shoes allow the sprinter the freedom she needs to dash to the finish line. Electricians rely on the thick rubber soles of their shoes to conduct electricity through and out of their bodies should they unfortunately touch live, crossed wires. We wear galoshes in the rain and fur-lined boots in the snow.

Many sports and occupations have specialized shoes that allow the participants to be involved with ease and confidence. Spiritually speaking, if your feet are covered with peace, you will walk through your Christian life with confidence as well.

However, again we run into Satan and the normal vicissitudes of life, all intent upon tripping us up. How? By supplying us with the opposite of ease and confidence, specifically, by interjecting *disease*. Our Power Suit shoes will not fit until we determinedly take off "the other shoes," meaning the ways we're used to handling our circumstances.

What Hampers the Fit of Peace Shoes?

The famous biblical parable of the sower and the seed recorded in Mark, chapter 4, discusses how people in various life situations receive the Word of God. Verses 18 and 19 tell us that when the seed (the Word) falls among thorns, *"the worries of this life, the deceitfulness of wealth and the desires for other things come in and choke the word, making it unfruitful."* These verses actually set up the main three situations that block our peace. We're either consumed by the worries of this life (stressed out), chasing deceitful wealth (strung out), or coveting rather than acting in faith (sapped out). So, in keeping with God's comparison of needing the right kind of shoes to accentuate the Power Suit, let's couple these three situations with three wrong kinds of shoes we are wearing that block the proper fit of the shoes of peace.

Stressed Out in the Strappy Sandals of Stress

The first way in which our peace is destroyed is by stress. Although it's impossible to avoid stress entirely, because life just happens, we can control our response to it.

According to *Merriam-Webster* online, *stress* is "a physical, chemical, or emotional factor that causes bodily or mental tension and may be a factor in disease causation." Look at that: stress affects us physically, chemically, and emotionally. Stress upsets our personal balance. The Holmes-Rahe Life Stress Inventory lists the top ten stressful life events as follows:

1. Spouse's death
2. Divorce
3. Marriage separation
4. Jail term
5. Death of a close relative
6. Injury or illness
7. Marriage
8. Fired from job
9. Marriage reconciliation
10. Retirement

In addition to these top ten, basically anything that upsets our equilibrium is considered a stressor. Issues like money worries, workplace pressures, a new baby, being overscheduled, your child's discipline problems, and even terrible traffic are all stress-producers. We're also stressed by different things; that which stresses me won't necessarily be a stressor for you.

I liken stress to strappy sandals, because when we step into it, we get it all over us. Think of how you'd feel if you stepped into fresh dog poop while wearing strappy sandals. Repulsed, right? The stuff is not only on your shoes, but it's also on your feet, and now you must use your hands to clean yourself up. You turn your nose up at the smell, and your eyes begin to look about frantically for anything to help you get the poop off of you. Your entire attention is turned to the dilemma. Stress affects us in the same way. When we step in it, our entire attention is turned to get us through or out of the situation.

An article entitled "Understanding Stress" at www.helpguide.org provided an excellent chart of the cognitive, emotional, physical, and behavioral warning signs and symptoms of stress, well worth searching and reading. Why? We are struggling with these symptoms because we attempt to face the cares of this world (stressors) in our own power—while wearing strappy sandals—rather than to approach stressors wearing the shoes of peace.

> We are struggling with these symptoms because we attempt to face the cares of this world in our own power.

In Luke 10:38–42, we read about Martha who was stressed by her busyness. She manifested her stressed state by allowing her frustration to explode into a complaint against her sister. Jesus tells Martha that she was anxious, distracted, and bothered by many things, all of which were not the most necessary. It wasn't so much that Martha should not be doing the cooking. The problem was her concentration on that to the exclusion of the attention she should have been paying to Jesus. Like many of us, Martha was more concerned with work than with worship, and this is how she missed the point and ended up stepping into the poop of stress.

Ladies, basically this passage is giving us profound advice about handling stress. First, replace the strappy sandals with peace shoes. We find peace at Jesus' feet. We find peace in worship. Listen as the Psalms tell us about worship.

PSALM 5:7 *"But I, by your great mercy, will come into your house; in reverence will I bow down toward your holy temple."* We are worshipping God when we approach Him reverently and respectfully. We find peace in worship as we recognize our position in relation to God's. He is God and sovereign, and we are His servants; not the other way around. It is not worship, and we are not living peaceably with God if we think we can order God around. God's not a cosmic bellhop, existing to fulfill our demands. We exist to do His will.

PSALM 22:29 *"All the rich of the earth will feast and worship."* We are worshipping God when we remember that God has supplied our blessings. We find peace when we are enjoying the good things in life and we don't forget from whose hand those good things flow.

PSALM 66:4 *"'All the earth bows down to you; they sing praise to you, they sing praise to your name.' Selah."* We worship God through singing. We find peace by keeping God on our minds and singing songs of worship allows God-thoughts to flow through our hearts.

PSALM 95:6 *"Come, let us bow down in worship, let us kneel before the LORD our Maker."*

PSALM 96:9 *"Worship the LORD in the splendor of his holiness; tremble before him, all the earth."* We are worshipping God when we live holy lives. He is holy so we must strive for holiness. We find peace in obedience, in doing what is right. A life lived in submission and obedience to God is a life lived without fear of repercussions from earthly authorities like the police, our bosses, our teachers, etc. This brings God glory.

PSALM 97:6–7 *"The heavens proclaim his righteous-ness, and all the peoples see his glory. All who worship images are put to shame, those who boast in idols—worship* *him, all you gods!"* We are worshipping God when we shun idols. We find peace as we direct our worship to the one true God rather than directing our worship to money, material goods, our mate, or anything else that seeks to take God's place in our lives.

PSALM 138:2 *"I will bow down toward your holy temple and will praise your name for your love and your faithfulness, for you have exalted above all things your name and your word."* We are worshipping God when we exalt His name and His Word because He has exalted His name and His Word above everything else. We find peace as we invoke His name in our times of stress. We also find peace as we hold His Word up as the final authority in all our outlooks and decisions.

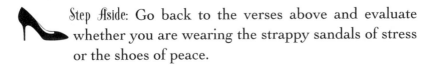 Step Aside: Go back to the verses above and evaluate whether you are wearing the strappy sandals of stress or the shoes of peace.

1. (Psalm 5:7) Do you insist that God do what you ask (tell) Him to do, or do you approach Him reverently realizing you exist to serve Him?

2. (Psalm 22:29*a*) Are you always mindful of the source of your blessings?

3. (Psalm 66:4) Do you sing worship songs to the Lord?

4. (Psalm 95:6 and 96:9) Are you living a holy life?

5. (Psalm 97:7–8) Are you directing your worship to God, or are you worshipping some kind of idol?

6. (Psalm 138:2) Do you lift up God's name and look to the Bible as the final authority for every viewpoint you hold and every decision you make?

Strung Out in the High Heels of Haughtiness

Referring back to the parable of the sower in the Gospel of Mark, the second thing that steals our peace is the deceitfulness

We all need money to live, but we're speaking here of an obsession with thinking that money can buy peace; it can't.

of wealth. I have likened the deceitfulness of wealth to high heels, because both can make us unstable if our dependence is on them without using any other kind of wisdom.

When we're walking on three- or four-inch heels, our gait can be unsteady. We can easily misstep, twist an ankle, or fall. We're spending so much time and energy trying to be cute and walk in these things without stumbling, that we could miss out on taking part in other things going on around us. One famous talk-show hostess, who sits through most of her programs, remarked that her gorgeous high heels were for looking at, not for walking or standing in for any length of time.

Chasing riches makes us unsteady as well. True, we all need money to live, but we're speaking here of an obsession with thinking that money can buy peace, and it can't. We figure, *If I just had more money, I could…*, or *if I just had more money, I would be….* You may even know some people who expressed those thoughts, and then changed when they actually got money. They got all puffed up, and basically, full of themselves. That's because they ascribed to money the power to make them new and different. Now that they have it, they face the new problems of keeping it and keeping it away from those who would deceitfully use them to get it. On the other hand, we've all heard of people who committed suicide, believing they had nothing left to live for when they unexpectedly lost all of their money.

Having money doesn't solve problems, nor does it make us good and peaceful people. Money is only a tool to be used with wisdom and discretion. The riches themselves are not the problem. God specifically tells us that it's our attitude toward the riches that causes all the upset. First Timothy 6:10 lays it on the line saying, *"For the love of money is a root of all kinds of evil. Some people, eager for money, have wandered from the faith and pierced themselves with many griefs."*

The rich young ruler of Matthew 19:16–22 was wearing the high heels of haughtiness when he met face-to-face with Jesus one day. He figured he was perfect and wanted Jesus to affirm that belief. The guy asked Jesus what good thing he had to do to inherit eternal life. Jesus told him to obey the Commandments. The fellow insisted that Jesus enumerate which ones he had to obey, so Jesus listed six that covered the young man's relationship with others; namely, *"Do not murder, do not commit adultery, do not steal, do not give false testimony, honor your father and mother, and love your neighbor as yourself"* (v. 19).

Hearing this answer, the guy felt pretty good about himself, so he pushed to hear Jesus tell him he was perfect and said, *"All these I have kept . . . What do I still lack?"* (v. 20).

Jesus then told him what he hadn't expected to hear. *"If you want to be perfect, go, sell your possessions and give to the poor, and you will have treasure in heaven. Then come, follow me"* (v. 21).

Yikes. This was inconceivable to him. This fellow was so into his money that his claim to fame is being the only man singled out in Scripture who was invited to become a disciple, yet refused because of his wealth. He allowed his money to deceive him into thinking his stature was more important than his service to the Master.

And therein lies the danger of the deceitfulness of riches. We, too, can be duped into believing that chasing the almighty dollar and maintaining our stature in society is more important than spending time with the Savior and pursuing our relationship with Him. In Ecclesiastes 5:10, the richest, wisest man who ever lived shares these words, *"Whoever loves money never has money enough; whoever loves wealth is never satisfied with his income. This too is meaningless."*

The shoes of peace will only replace the high heels of haughtiness if we focus on relegating money, and the power we think it brings, to its proper place in our lives. We will be living in peace when we control money rather than letting money control us. When we get some, we must be careful and responsible with it so that our use of it is pleasing to God. Proverbs 28:20 backs up this point. *"A faithful man will be richly blessed, but one eager to get rich will not go unpunished."*

 Step Aside: Are you wearing the high heels of haughtiness and chasing after the deceitfulness of riches, or are you outfitted in the shoes of peace? Read the following verses and respond honestly to the questions that follow them.

JEREMIAH 9:23–24

Do you boast of your riches?
Are you more apt to learn about handling money or to understand more about God?

MATTHEW 6:24

Who do you serve the most: God or money? (To answer this, consider where your time and attention are spent the most.)

HEBREWS 13:5

Are you content with what you have?

Sapped Out in the Flip-Flops of Faithlessness

If we're not stressed out by the worries of this life or strung out by haughtiness, the third way in which our peace is destroyed is by being strung out over the desire for things, coveting rather than acting in faith. I am likening this desire to flip-flops because when we're in this mindset, we flip-flop from dependence on one thing to dependence on something else, instead of exhibiting unshakable faith in God. As long as we're wearing flip-flops, the shoes of peace won't fit.

Peace shoes enable us to walk on "waves." Peter was wearing some in Matthew 14:22–33 when Jesus strolled across the wind-whipped water of the lake to catch up with the boat in which the disciples were sailing. Although startled by the sight of someone walking on water, after Jesus identified Himself, Peter called out, *"Lord, if it's you, tell me to come to you on the water."* When Jesus told him to come on, he did. The passage relates, *"Then Peter got down out of the boat, walked on the water and came toward Jesus. But when he saw the wind, he was afraid and, beginning to sink, cried out, 'Lord, save me!' Immediately Jesus reached out his hand and caught him. 'You of little faith,' he said, 'why did you doubt?' And when they climbed into the boat, the wind died down."*

This story gives us a clear outline of how to walk in peace shoes above the waves of stress. Watch what we can learn from Peter about becoming wave-walkers.

First, in the midst of Peter's storm, he set his focus above the waves. If Peter had concentrated his attention downward on the churning waves, he would have missed the approaching help. I know problems can be overwhelming, but we must deliberately lift our eyes and focus above them. Psalm 42:5 states plainly, *"Why are you downcast, O my soul? Why so disturbed within me? Put your hope in God, for I will yet praise him."* No matter what's going on around, Jesus does not desert us. (We'll

This story gives us a clear outline of how to walk in peace shoes, above the waves of stress.

talk more about this in chapter 5 when we discuss the shield of faith.)

What if Dr. Martin Luther King Jr. had kept his eyes focused on the churning waves of racism and the evil of segregation? He never would have been able to have, much less share with the world, his dream for a nation in which people would not be judged by the color of their skin but by the content of their character.

What if Corrie Ten Boom had kept her eyes focused on the storm of the Holocaust? She never would have been able to live through that hell to share with us that there is no pit so deep that our God is not deeper still.

What if Mother Teresa had kept her eyes focused only on the winds of poverty all around her? She never would have comforted thousands and arrested the attention of the world, awakening us to our planet's problems of the crushing needs of the poor.

These and so many others looked above the waves whipped up by the storms they faced and were able to see help coming from God, even if they didn't experience complete fulfillment in their lifetimes.

Second, even though Peter looked above the waves for help, he was a bit wary to jump at the help he saw coming. He checked to be sure it was Jesus coming toward him. When we are stressed, we're wearing flip-flops if we look to any other help but Jesus.

Stressful situations easily cause us to panic and hurry to accept a quick fix or the first relief that comes along. It's understandable to seek to shorten our suffering as much as possible; however, wisdom dictates that we exercise caution, especially when we feel harried. That's when we make rash decisions. The shoes of peace will only supply that peace to us if we check to be sure it's the Prince of Peace coming to our rescue.

Third, once Peter realized he was indeed speaking with Jesus, he made his request. Notice something: Peter had so accepted the problem of the raging wind that he didn't ask Jesus to stop it. He simply asked to go to Jesus on the waves. Peter's prayer could be restated, "Lord, if You call me to You, I will walk on top of my stress."

The requests we make of God in our times of trouble are all important. If we center our requests on God's glory rather than on our greed, we'll find ourselves as wave-walkers. Think of Solomon. When he faced the stress of taking over as king, he asked God not for power or riches, but for wisdom to govern the Israelite people. God was so pleased with that request, He not only granted it, but added blessings to it.

Finally, Peter became a wave-walker when he followed Jesus' directive in Jesus' way. Jesus told Peter to come to Him, so Peter stepped over the side of the rocking boat, out onto the boisterous water, and took steps. Nothing changed about Peter's current reality but his attitude toward it. Obeying Jesus meant an immediate redirection of his attention and thereby, a release from stress.

Peter wavered slightly, ruining his peace, by taking his eyes off of Jesus, but he had good enough sense to look quickly back to Jesus, grab on to His hand, and then wave-walk together with Jesus once again.

By donning the shoes of peace, we, too, will walk above the waves that seek to rock our boat. As long as we keep our eyes on Jesus and our concentration on what Jesus has said, we can be at peace, even though we are well aware of stormy circumstances surrounding us.

 Step Aside: Are you wearing the flip-flops of faithlessness or the shoes of peace? When facing any kind of stressful situation, use Peter's four-step program to wave-walk.

1. Set your focus above the waves.

   Make a deliberate decision to raise your sights above your stress. Do not become irresponsible, but a redirection of your attention will lead to a realignment of your attitude.

   Identify your specific stressors. List them. For each stressor, write down at least one way you can realign your focus.

2. Check to be sure your help is coming from Jesus.

   To whom have you looked for help? Are those helpers giving you advice based upon biblical truth?

3. Make the right request.

   Instead of the prayer that says, *"God, please get me out of this mess,"* what can you request of God despite your situation that will bring Him glory?

4. Step out onto the waves.

   Make your move. With your eyes steadfastly fastened on Jesus, step out in faith.

A Real World Example

I hear you thinking, *Now all of this sounds good, but how does this pan out in a real life situation?* I'm glad you asked. It worked for my friend, BJ Jensen.

Becoming an entertainer who could sing, dance, and act was truly a focus set above the waves for BJ because she was born crippled and then was affected by polio at age ten. The reality of both her physical limitations and her tone-deafness stifled those aspirations. Despite those challenges, though, BJ's subdued creative juices continued to flow, and as she approached her 52nd birthday, she accepted a position to develop and direct a drama program at her church.

When given the opportunity to enhance her work by attending the Christian Artists' Seminar in the Rockies that was held at Estes Park, BJ jumped at the chance. Thousands of Christian artists would be assembled for competition, training, and nightly entertainment. God miraculously supplied the finances, and she knew she'd learn much to take back to her church program, but she wasn't prepared for what God also had in store.

"Dance for me in the competition." The thought of dancing in public at her age and size seemed almost comical to her. Was that really Jesus whispering to her? She checked through prayer and felt sure. She wanted to be obedient, but was terrified.

Asking God to help her obey, BJ entered the competition. The music started, she stepped out onto her waves, and she danced. To her amazement, she actually won the competition and danced her testimony before an audience of 3,000 at the closing concert of the conference.

She wanted to be obedient, but was terrified. She checked through prayer and felt sure.

Let's remember the steps once again:

Set your focus above the waves.

Check to be sure the help is coming from Jesus.

Make the right request.

Step out onto the waves.

The process works the same if you're facing physical or emotional health issues, financial turnaround, or estrangement from your spouse or child. The shoes of peace will enable you to walk on your waves.

What God Will Do

When your feet are shod with the preparation of the gospel of peace, you are trusting God to handle the turmoil in your life. God takes hold of your hand; He directs your steps. Walk where He says to walk and nowhere else. He will not take you anywhere He has not already been. He knows the lay of the land. No more need for stress; no fear of land mines. He has either cleared the mines, or He'll walk you around them.

Habakkuk 3:19, expertly discussed in *Matthew Henry's Commentary*, speaks to the results of wearing the shoes of peace: *"The Sovereign LORD is my strength; he makes my feet like the feet of a deer, he enables me to go on the heights."* The commentary reflects, "We shall be strong for our spiritual warfare and work... We shall be swift for our spiritual race... We shall be successful in our spiritual enterprises."

You see, when we are following God as we should, He will set our feet in the right places, bend us like an archer bends his bow, and send us to the high places where He intends for us to go. God has special plans and special high places designed individually and personally for each one of us. Are we pliable? Are we flexible enough in His hands that He will be able to bend us, aim us, and shoot us to where we have to go when it's time for us to go? Even if life's circumstances are not happy ones, we are wearing the shoes of peace when our feet are treading in the place God wants us to be.

Step Aside: Reflecting on the truths discussed in this chapter about wearing the shoes of peace, journal a prayer of rejoicing after reading the following verses:

Philippians 4:13
Matthew 6:30
Mark 9:23

Section 3
Faith and Salvation

Chapter 5

Convertible Carryall

The Shield of Faith

From the comfort of our den, my husband and I watched on TV the horrors of hurricanes slamming into the southern and eastern coasts of the United States. We prayed for the people of New Orleans as we watched them suffering through the devastation of Katrina. We kept tabs by cell phone on our youngest son, Mark, as he evacuated from Southern University ahead of Gustav. And we maintained phone contact with Jean, my husband's sister, as she rode out Ike in her home in Houston.

In each crisis, the difference between death and survival was directly related to *preparedness*. Thanks to satellite imagery, meteorologists are able to broadcast warnings well in advance. Those who were able to do so heeded the warnings and removed themselves from harm's way. In other words, those who had faith in the alerts, acted by either getting out of Dodge or doing whatever it would take to protect themselves as they hunkered down to ride things out. People either moved or prepared, even though the skies were clear and it wasn't even raining yet.

Away from the crisis, it's easy to become critical. We could have had harsh thoughts of those who heard the hurricane warnings, were able to evacuate, and yet did not, and because of their stubbornness, they either died or forced rescue workers to put their lives in peril to assist them.

Although we don't live in a hurricane zone, we can be just as guilty of ignoring important warnings. James and I live in Southern California—earthquake country. Whenever the earth feels the urge, those tectonic plates suddenly widen, slide, or smash into each other. Because of the inevitability of such events in our region, earthquake preparedness seminars are offered at which we can learn what's needed if "the big one" strikes. Then we're expected to go home, gather together the necessary items in a box, and store that box someplace where we'll not only remember it, but be able to get to it in the case of an earthquake emergency.

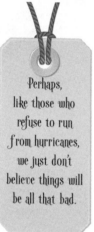

Perhaps, like those who refuse to run from hurricanes, we just don't believe things will be all that bad.

Do most of us in Southern California have an earthquake box? No. Why not? Out of sight; out of mind. Perhaps like those who refuse to run from hurricanes, we just don't believe things will be that bad. Even after a sizeable tremor that knocks pictures off shelves and considerably rattles our nerves, as the days pass, we forget about it. Pretty soon, we move on quickly from telling the where-I-was-when-the-ground-shook stories to relating the more pressing issues of the moment. Most of us don't even think of it again until we're running for a door jamb or diving under a table because the ground is rocking and rolling once again.

Spiritually speaking, the difference between defeat (death) and success (survival) is also directly related to preparedness. Thanks to the Word of God, the biblical writers have broadcast divine warnings in advance. Those who are willing and able to do so heed the warnings and remove themselves from harm's way. In other words, those who have faith in God's Word—His alerts—act on what He says, even though the situational skies look clear at the time.

The shield of faith affords us protection in the same manner in which hurricane warnings do. By carrying the shield, we are ready to face the oncoming assaults of the enemy, no matter what form those assaults may take; however, we forget about the protection of the shield in much the same way as when we let hurricane warnings and earthquake preparedness slip. God's Word tells us what we need to watch out for; it tells us what's coming. We are accessing the power of the shield when, by faith, we believe and act in advance of the problem.

Picture a large garden labyrinth you can literally navigate through on foot. The hedge walls are too tall to see over, so you must walk blindly up and down the paths, not knowing when you will come to a dead end and have to backtrack. Now imagine that a close friend of yours is perched high above the maze, able to see both the entrance and the exit. She can even see the dead ends.

She starts calling to you and saying things like, "Turn right around the next hedge."

"Pass the next opening, and walk straight until you can turn left."

"Take an immediate right, then pass two lanes before you take another right turn."

If you start arguing with her, she could just reassure you by responding, "Trust me on this."

Would it make sense for you to ignore your friend's directions? Of course not. Why not? Because she has the advantage of seeing the end result of turns you cannot see. As long as you have faith in your friend's directions, you will avoid getting stopped, stuck, and frustrated. Holding up the shield of faith is like listening to that friend. If we listen and heed, we breeze through.

Now picture a second person perched above the labyrinth beside your friend. This person seems intelligent. In fact, this person eruditely calls out different messages that distract you from giving your full attention to your friend. If you let it, you could even allow this second voice to drown out the first voice.

The problem is, as sweet and persuasive as this second voice sounds, the personality behind it is bent on being sure you do not exit the maze. If you listen to the second voice, you could end up dying in a cul-de-sac.

The voice of your friend represents God's voice, the second voice represents Satan's voice, the labyrinth represents life, and your obedience to the directions of the first voice represents listening to God and using the shield of faith. As you listen to God, you activate your faith, and you, thereby, ward off any and every attack Satan throws your way. You literally shield yourself from the enemy's onslaught. Come along as we dig deeper into this shield idea.

Break Down the Verse

Let's analyze the verse that deals with this part of the Power Suit—the shield of faith: *"In addition to all this, take up the shield of faith, with which you can extinguish all the flaming arrows of the evil one"* (Ephesians 6:16).

Q: After surrounding yourself with truth, putting on righteousness, and sliding on the shoes of peace, what are we to do next?
A: Take up the shield of faith.

Q: What does "take up" mean?
A: The Greek word *analambano* is really a combination of two Greek words: *ana*[ah-nah], which when used in compounds means repetition and intensity; and *lambano* [lahm-BAH-no], which means to get hold of. Take up, then, means to volitionally and repetitiously take into your hands. So, taking up the shield is an act of our will. This direction is given by a loving Father who knows what's best for us but who gives us the freedom to make our own choices because we are grown.

Q: What is the purpose of the shield of faith?
A: To extinguish, put out, render useless and ineffective, flaming arrows.

Q: What are flaming arrows?
A: "The fiery darts (or flaming arrows) that were used in war (back in biblical days) were small, slender pieces of cane, which were filled with combustible materials, and set on fire... and then shot "slowly" against a foe. The object was to make the arrow fasten in the body, and increase the danger by the burning; or, more frequently, those darts were thrown against ships, forts, tents, etc., with an intention to set them on fire.... Paul here refers, probably, to the temptations of the great adversary, which are like fiery darts; or those furious suggestions of evil, and excitements to sin, which he may throw into the mind like fiery darts. They are—blasphemous thoughts, unbelief, sudden temptation to do wrong, or thoughts that wound and torment the soul" (from *Barnes' Notes*).

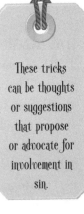

These tricks can be thoughts or suggestions that propose or advocate for involvement in sin.

In other words, the flaming arrows are the tricks of Satan thrown at us to set us on fire; literally, to inflame, provoke, and agitate us. These tricks can be thoughts or suggestions that propose or advocate for involvement in sin. Once the thought is planted (that's the arrow part), continuing to think on it acts as a slow burn (that's the fiery part) and eventually ignites in our carrying out the act.

I'm reminded of what I've heard about the use of napalm during the Vietnam conflict. As if the explosion of the bomb were not enough, on impact, napalm would be released from the casing and would shower upon anyone and anything around. Napalm acted like acid, and although a person survived the bomb blast, he would suffer in agony as his skin burned off of his bones.

So it is with flaming arrows. You think you've survived the thought, but the commitment of the sin borne by that thought leads to pain, suffering, and ultimately, death.

Q: Who is responsible for the arrows?
A: The evil one—Satan.

Q: What can be done about the arrows?
A: The arrows can be extinguished by our use of the shield of faith.

The word *extinguish* comes from the Greek word *sbennumi* [SBEN-new-mee], which means to put out, quench, squash, or resist. There is not a promise in our verse that says the flaming arrows won't come at us; however, the danger is averted by our use of the shield of faith.

Q: So who has the biggest stake in keeping us from avoiding those arrows?
A: The evil one—Satan.

Q: So, doesn't it make sense then to evaluate Satan's tactics to see how he plans to keep us from using the shield?
A: Yes!

In the grand scheme of things, our adversary, the devil, is a master at being that second voice we spoke of earlier in our labyrinth example. It is to his advantage to distract us because when we stop listening to God, our shield comes down. A lowered shield means a vulnerable warrior. The enemy can attack. He can destroy us—kill us—in the maze of the vicissitudes of this life.

Exactly how then does the devil get us to lower our shield of faith? He distracts us by filling our hands with other stuff we have to hold, stuff other than the shield of faith. These things are in the way, thus allowing those flaming arrows to get to us.

Let's examine six ways Satan prevents us from using the shield of faith. He uses irritation, immoderation, self-absorption, complication, distraction, and diversion.

Irritation

The first way Satan moves to prevent us from using the shield of faith is by causing irritation. What kind of irritation? He tries to keep us all upset and irritated with each other. Second Corinthians 2:10–11 says, *"If you forgive anyone, I also forgive him. And what I have forgiven—if there was anything to forgive—I have forgiven in the sight of Christ for your sake, in order that Satan might not outwit us. For we are not unaware of his schemes"* (emphasis added). For the last part of that verse, the King James Version says, *"Lest Satan should get an advantage of us: for we are not ignorant of his devices."*

There's a lot of confusion out there concerning forgiveness.

You see, the only reason we would have the need to forgive someone is if we feel that person has done something against us. This verse is saying that it's important for us to forgive, because living in unforgiveness is how Satan outwits us or takes advantage of us. God's love is not flowing through us if we do not forgive. If God is not flowing, our shield is down.

There's a lot of confusion out there concerning forgiveness. Let's put to rest one very common misconception. You've probably heard it said that for true forgiveness to exist, it's necessary to "forgive and forget." Loud buzzer; wrong answer.

Like omniscience and omnipresence, the ability to forgive and forget is one of God's attributes. The Bible tells us, *"As far as the east is from the west, so far has he removed our transgressions from us"* (Psalm 103:12). We do not take on God's divine attributes, but we can take on His character. Our brains may not forget offenses, but our hearts can forgive them. Our brains are wired to work with our common sense and steer our bodies clear of harm's way, but our regenerated hearts can yield to God's directives on forgiveness and release offenders from our personal wrath and bitterness.

You see, forgiveness does not erase guilt nor does it necessarily release the offender from punishment. Forgiveness releases a person from our judging grasp, firmly placing him or her into God's hands. And knowing that we are God's precious daughters, we hear God saying out of love for us, *"Do not take revenge, my friends, but leave room for God's wrath, for it is written: 'It is mine to avenge; I will repay,' says the Lord"* (Romans 12:19). In essence, God is saying, "What? Somebody is messing with you? No worries. You just move on with your life. You do believe I can handle this, don't you? Let Me work."

My friend Gloria* lived this out after her divorce. Her ex-husband had been unfaithful and abusive, so for the sake of her sanity, and for her and her daughters' safety, she ended the marriage. After several years, she met and married Philip, who treated them all like priceless jewels.

The one thing Philip couldn't figure out, though, was why Gloria wasn't much more upset with her ex when he still did and said ridiculous things. Philip was especially disturbed to realize that the man did nothing significant for his three little girls. Gloria had to explain to Philip that continuing to stress out over her ex's shortcomings would only keep her inextricably attached to him emotionally. She had let him go, which meant forgiving him and releasing him into God's hands for whatever God deemed just.

As the years passed, Gloria, Philip, and the girls' lives flourished, but as Gloria's ex-husband refused to grow past his shortcomings, his life spiraled into worse and worse disrepair. At last report, he had succumbed to a debilitating medical condition that makes his everyday existence quite difficult.

Whether it's a former husband, bothersome coworker, irksome sibling, or nosy in-law—whoever is causing the confusion—we simply must stop being constantly irritated with each other. Forgive. Release people. They may see the value in reconciliation, but if they don't, move on. Relational irritation keeps our eyes focused horizontally rather than vertically. We hold these irritations instead of the shield of faith in our hands and then can't understand why we're fiery-dart plagued.

Step Aside: Are you harboring unforgiveness in your heart toward anyone? If so, meditate on Mark 11:24–25:

"Therefore I tell you, whatever you ask for in prayer, believe that you have received it, and it will be yours. And when you stand praying, if you hold anything against anyone, forgive him, so that your Father in heaven may forgive you your sins."

What is God saying to you through these verses?

In light of our present conversation, reflect on the following verses. How does each one relate to a situation that is irritating you? Don't forget to confess your contribution to the irritations.

PSALM 7:9 *O righteous God, who searches minds and hearts, bring to an end the violence of the wicked and make the righteous secure.*

JEREMIAH 17:10 *"I the LORD search the heart and examine the mind, to reward a man according to his conduct, according to what his deeds deserve."*

PSALM 145:20 *The LORD watches over all who love him, but all the wicked he will destroy.*

PSALM 34:19 *A righteous man may have many troubles, but the LORD delivers him from them all.*

Immoderation

The second way Satan prevents us from using the shield of faith is through our immoderation; in other words, he has us believe we can live any kind of way and still be teachers, preachers, and proclaimers of the gospel. Loud buzzer; wrong again.

Philippians 4:5 (KJV) debunks this idea. *"Let your moderation be known unto all men. The Lord is at hand."* Moderation comes from the Greek word *epieikes* [epp-ee-aa-KASE], which is defined as "appropriate, mild, gentle, and patient behavior." This Greek word is further broken down into two Greek roots that mean "be like, but above." Simply stated, our appropriate, mild, gentle, and patient ways should so stand out that people recognize Christ in us. Satan wants us to conform to the culture so no one can tell the difference between us and nonbelievers.

We are not using the shield of faith when we are immoderate. When our manner of life does not honor God, we leave ourselves open to fiery-dart attacks. For example, when speaking to a lonely, single friend, how can we witness to the power of God to bless our obedience if we are stuck in fornication ourselves? Are we good illustrations of God's ability to meet our needs if we refuse to tithe and remain trapped in credit-card debt?

Read 2 Corinthians 4:1–7 and we'll discuss this idea further.

> *Therefore, since through God's mercy we have this ministry, we do not lose heart. Rather, we have renounced secret and shameful ways; we do not use deception, nor do we distort the Word of God. On the contrary, by setting forth the truth plainly we commend ourselves to every man's conscience in the sight of God. And even if our gospel is veiled, it is veiled to those who are perishing. The god of this age has blinded the minds of unbelievers, so that they cannot see the light of the gospel of the glory of Christ, who is the image of God. For we do not preach ourselves, but Jesus Christ as Lord, and ourselves as your servants for Jesus' sake. For God, who said, "Let light shine out of darkness," made his light shine in our*

hearts to give us the light of the knowledge of the glory of God in the face of Christ. But we have this treasure in jars of clay to show that this all-surpassing power is from God and not from us.

So, exactly how can we live in moderation, and thus throw up the shield of faith against Satan's darts that would seek to destroy us in this area? We must renounce secret and shameful ways, not use deception, and not distort of Word of God, setting forth the truth plainly, commending ourselves to every man's conscience in the sight of God.

California became the 30th state to vote down the acceptance of homosexual marriage, when the citizenry were first given the opportunity to vote on this issue in 2008 and when the measure failed to make it onto the ballot to lift the ban in 2010. State after state had affirmed that the majority of Americans want the definition of marriage to remain as being between one man and one woman. Judges are trying to override the desire of the people, but on this issue, the majority remained steadfast in renouncing the *"secret and shameful ways"* of the homosexual lifestyle. (See 1 Corinthians 6:9–10; Romans 1:26–27; and Leviticus 18:22.)

It is our responsibility as children of God to openly renounce secret and shameful ways. We start first with our personal lifestyle and then move into the culture. I must stop lying, cheating, stealing, fornicating, gossiping, lusting, coveting, killing, and so on. Then I must gently speak up for God's standards to be set forth in the culture. All laws have their basis in morality; they are an expression of what is deemed right or wrong. God alone sets those standards and our laws are to then reflect those standards. The argument that religion should not affect culture is moot. We legislate morality all the time; we will go to prison for robbing a bank, kidnapping, and even for brandishing a weapon because these things are morally wrong.

Laws might not change hearts, but they should not force us to approve of lawbreakers. Criminals are in jail because they did something morally wrong; they broke the law and were judged.

Even those who still hold that we cannot legislate morality need to flip the script and notice that we must not legislate in favor of immorality. The renouncing of secret and shameful ways starts with our admission of having them.

Step Aside: Are there any secret and shameful ways in your life that you need to renounce? Find Bible verses that deal with your specific issue, meditate on them, and pray for God's help to change.

Are there any secret and shameful ways you have seen around you that you have approved of either by verbal assent or by silence? Again, by using the Bible, discover God's mind about this specific issue and look for loving ways to mention how God feels about this. Ask for the Holy Spirit's guidance as to how far into the public square He wants you to take it.

In addition to renouncing secret and shameful ways, the second way to live in moderation is to stop using deception. Satan is the master deceiver, known as the father of lies (John 8:44) so he's great at tempting us to participate here.

Have you noticed how easy it is to lie? Lies just roll off of the tongue like honey. Some of us are really smooth at it too. My friend Kathleen* sent me an insightful confession about lying:

Before the knowledge of God, lying was simply a method of survival. Lies aided my daily life. When I didn't have the money to pay for the newspaper or insurance, I would tell my children to answer the phone and tell the collectors, "Mommy isn't home." I had no understanding that lying is actually manipulation. More importantly, I didn't realize I was teaching my children to lie to avoid responsibility for their actions or to get what they wanted.

Yet, I hated lies when they were used against me. I lost a job with a lawyer once because I refused to lie and say I was responsible for his slack in failing to adequately prepare a legal document. Somehow, I differentiated between my lies as little white lies that were necessary for survival and the big lies that hurt people.

Of course, God calls a lie a lie.

And once an action is taught, it becomes habit. My children learned well. I'm ashamed of how great a job I did passing along this ungodly trait. Throughout one son's career, he admits he often lied because he perceived things never worked out when he told the truth. My other son paid a horrible price. He spent almost half of his life in prison having refused to heed my advice to achieve success through honest work. Why wouldn't he listen to me? He told me he couldn't trust me, his mom the liar, in his earlier years because my actions didn't match my words.

My children paid the price for what I never intended to teach them. Now I look to our merciful and forgiving God to fix what I messed up. I'm praying that He is working in my children to dig up and destroy those lying roots that have grown from the seeds I unwittingly planted.

As deceivers, we let down the shield of faith and set ourselves up as fiery-arrow targets. Remember that Satan is lurking.

As deceivers, we let down the shield of faith and set ourselves up as fiery-arrow targets. Remember that Satan is lurking in the shadows, seeking an opportunity to destroy us. All that's necessary is for us to be caught in one lie and the rest of our character is seriously called into question. And depending upon the magnitude of the lie, or the people who catch us lying, we might be setting ourselves up for very dire consequences.

Jesus said, *"If you hold to my teaching, you are really my disciples. Then you will know the truth, and the truth will set you free'"* (John 8:31–32). We douse Satan's fiery arrows when we live by God's truth. Put deception down; pick up the shield of faith. No need to lie. When we live in God's truth there is nothing to hide. Satan will have no skeletons to expose. (And always remember: skeletons have no muscle.)

Step Aside: When do you lie? Why? What can you do to stop lying?

The third way to live in moderation is to steer clear of distorting the Word of God. Our job must be, as the 2 Corinthians 4 passage above reminds us, to set forth the truth plainly, commending ourselves to everyone's conscience in the sight of God. Just be honest about God's Word and real about our relationship to it.

It is especially tempting to distort God's Word in our culture of tolerance. This mind-set took a foothold in the late 1960s with the explosion of the best-selling book by Thomas A. Harris entitled *I'm OK—You're OK*. Contrary to the book's notion that we're all great and right no matter what we do, according to Scripture, I'm *not* OK, and you're *not* OK either. This accept-everything mentality continued through my junior and senior high school years during the 1970s. School psychology classes taught us about situation ethics: what's right may change based upon the situation.

Well, just as we discussed morality a little earlier, the above notions are bogus. We distort God's Word if we hold to the situation ethics model. God's Word is clear, *"For all have sinned and fall short of the glory of God"* (Romans 3:23), and *"As it is written: 'There is no one righteous, not even one'"* (Romans 3:10). When we refuse to hold and live by God's position on issues that He clearly outlines in the Bible, we distort God's Word. Others see us living contrary to the Word of God and have a clear conscience when they do the same thing. After all, the Christian examples (us) are doing it, so it must be OK with God.

Bottom line: The shield of faith is held high when our hearts are open to change our ways—live in moderation and line up with the Word of God—because other people are looking for Christ in us. Satan cannot get me with the fiery dart that screams, "Why do others have to live by God's standards; you don't."

Step Aside: What do the following verses tell you about how God feels about His people leading others into sin?

PROVERBS 28:10 *He who leads the upright along an evil path will fall into his own trap, but the blameless will receive a good inheritance.*

LUKE 17:1–3 *Jesus said to His disciples: "Things that cause people to sin are bound to come, but woe to that person through whom they come. It would be better for him to be thrown into the sea with a millstone tied around his neck than for him to cause one of these little ones to sin. So watch yourselves. If your brother sins, rebuke him, and if he repents, forgive him."*

Self-Absorption

The third way Satan prevents us from using the shield of faith is through our self-absorption; that is, he wants us to fix our eyes on ourselves rather than on God, especially if we are proclaiming His Word in any way. When we're self-absorbed, we get so wrapped up in ourselves that we think our personal charisma, rather than the power of God, is causing the difference we see in people's lives. To add to the deception, Satan clouds the vision of the people to whom we are ministering so they think the differences are coming from us as well.

The November 26 entry in Oswald Chambers's *My Utmost for His Highest* speaks to this point:

> *"If I talk my own talk, it is of no more importance to you than your talk is to me; but if I talk the truth of God, you will meet it again and so will I. We have to concentrate on the great point of spiritual energy — the Cross, to keep in contact with that center where all the power lies, and the energy will be let loose."*

You see, when we are self-absorbed, our talk focuses on us—what we've started, what we've finished, what we've spearheaded, who we know, and who knows us. We're holding all these trophies in our hands, polishing and displaying them at every opportunity. There's no room in our hands for the shield of faith, now is there? And what happens when we are holding other things besides the shield of faith? That's right; we're fiery-dart sitting ducks.

Whenever we were a little more proud of ourselves than we should have been, my mother would quote Benjamin Franklin and tell us, "A man wrapped up in himself makes a very small bundle." God's light can shine through our hearts even though we are mere clay vessels. We cannot let our own clay grab all of our attention.

 Step Aside: There's nothing wrong with great ideas and grand influence; however, we must be careful to be sure God always gets the glory. After all, He opened those doors and orchestrated those meetings.

Reflect on the following verses in light of this conversation on self-absorption. What's God saying to you through them?

1 TIMOTHY 4:16 *Watch your life and doctrine closely. Persevere in them, because if you do, you will save both yourself and your hearers.*

JOHN 7:18 *He who speaks on his own does so to gain honor for himself, but he who works for the honor of the one who sent him is a man of truth; there is nothing false about him.*

JEREMIAH 9:23–24 *This is what the LORD says: "Let not the wise man boast of his wisdom or the strong man boast of his strength or the rich man boast of his riches, but let him who boasts boast about this: that he understands and knows me, that I am the LORD, who exercises kindness, justice and righteousness on earth, for in these I delight," declares the LORD.*

Complication

The fourth way Satan prevents us from using the shield of faith is by introducing complication into our relationship with Christ. He tries to make living for God seem complicated.

Second Corinthians 11:3 (KJV) states, *"But I fear, lest by any means, as the serpent beguiled Eve through his subtlety, so your minds should be corrupted from the simplicity that is in Christ."* God wants us to know Him. It doesn't make sense that God would make it difficult to understand how He expects us to live; nor is it conscionable that God would make it difficult for us to live as He asks. Would you request something of your children that they were utterly unable to do? Of course not. So it stands that it would be nonsensical for God to make living for Him complicated.

Satan tries to make living for God seem complicated.

Don't fall for the okeydoke. Satan has been using the complication technique in believer's lives since the beginning of time. As stated in the verse above, he started with Eve. In Genesis 3:1–5, he twisted his question to make Eve think God was withholding something valuable from her ("Did God really say...?"), then he complicated the issue by adding what sounded like reputable information ("For God knows...you will be like [Him], knowing good and evil"). Eve fell for it, let go of God, and we all know what happened next—a plunge into sin.

How does this complication trick work in our lives today? One term: *overcommitment.* We have our jobs, home and family responsibilities, schooling, hobbies, second jobs, church work, community volunteerism, and recreation. I'm sure I haven't named everything we feel obligated to do. With Eve, God had given her and Adam their clear job description: tend Eden and multiply. He never told them to explore the intricacies of good and evil. How many things are we doing that God never assigned to us?

This trick is driven by something I call "busyness addiction." Many of us feel as if we're wasting time if we're resting. There always has to be something going on. Multitasking has actually become our new religion. If we're not doing more than one thing at a time, we feel lazy, inadequate, and incomplete. Work, work, work. By the way, rest is a thing that needs to be done. Even God rested (remember the seventh day after Creation?).

This idea has crept into church. There are lots of really good things that need to be done. How many of us are in three or more auxiliaries? Why? Is there no one else in your entire congregation who can fill one of those spots? If you say no, my question is, How do you know? I bet if you die, someone else will either take your place or the spot will be retired, meaning it wasn't needed anyway.

This trick is driven by something I call "busyness addiction."

We are so tired after we have worked, held meetings, planned, conducted, driven, practiced, performed, and organized that we have no time left to listen to God, much less be involved in what He really wants us to do. If Satan can keep us busy with overcrowded schedules, we won't get around to operating in our God-given purpose. Our hands will be so full of appointments that there will be no room in them to hold up the shield of faith.

Proverbs 30:5–6 says, *"Every word of God is flawless; he is a shield to those who take refuge in him. Do not add to his words, or he will rebuke you and prove you a liar."* Listen only to God's instructions and make it your priority to accomplish what He says for you to do. Don't let Satan complicate your life with unnecessary activity. I've heard it said that whom God calls, He equips. It won't be stressful for you to know what God wants you to do and it won't be stressful for you to flourish while doing it.

Step Aside: Test yourself to see if you are a victim of unnecessary life complication. For one week, keep a detailed log of your activities hour by hour. At the end of the week, evaluate how you have been spending your time. Is there anything on that list that can or should be eliminated or delegated? Aside from everything involved with caring for yourself and your family, for each other activity on the list, ask yourself: *What would be the worse-case scenario if I stopped doing this?* Eliminate the unnecessary.

Distraction

The fifth way Satan prevents us from using the shield of faith is by introducing distraction. He raises up false teachers and then we follow their false doctrines.

Two of my friends, Myra* and Monica*, supplied me with a couple of examples about modern-day false teachers. Myra became curious about the many teachings claiming the ability to empower people to be all they could be. She became involved with an organization that required a $1,500 payment to enroll with the promise of success and certainty of being able to influence others' lives. She recognized some biblical principles interspersed with the ideas being taught. At completion of the first six-week program, she became eligible for the group's master's program, which included activities that took her even further away from true biblical doctrine as the bottom line of the teaching began to emerge: you are your own god.

Thanks to solid biblical teaching Myra had had in the past, she slowly began to come to herself and found that she was more confused and further away than ever from the life she really wanted, one that was pleasing to God. Myra says, "The group was like a cult. I learned a few good principles, but they were only the sugarcoating to distract me from the bad doctrine they were teaching."

Monica was attending a denominational church when the pastor attended a ministry meeting and returned from the sessions very excited about her new spiritual mentor. Never revealing any credentials, this mentor, Dr. Smithson* implied that she held greater spiritual truths than the bishop of the denomination. When Monica's pastor refused to break off the affiliation with this new mentor, the church split. Monica trusted in the pastor and felt the exposure to deeper spiritual teaching was helping her to grow, so she was one of 50 other members who followed the pastor to start a new church in a member's home.

Monica says, "I became less enchanted with the new church when manipulation and control tactics began operating at a drastic level. There were late-night phone calls designed to disrupt sleeping patterns, requirements for everyone to meet with the pastor to review all of their finances (under guise of teaching about tithing and budgeting), and pressure to socialize and vacation with other church members. Things became even stranger when Dr. Smithson died and truth about her lack of a doctorate and other facts became evident."

Why had Monica fallen into this deception? She told me she got caught up in the excitement and made the drastic mistake of following her pastor instead of the Holy Spirit. The strife caused by the church split and the wounds to the body of Christ in that congregation cannot be erased. So now Monica is very careful to be sure she is following the Lord and not a person or movement.

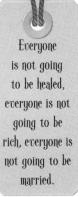

Everyone is not going to be healed, everyone is not going to be rich, everyone is not going to be married.

Second Peter 2:1–3 is a passage that discusses the fact that false teachers know they are teaching the wrong thing. They are bringing a bad name to all those who are teaching the right thing, and they are getting money out of people by doing it. We're admonished in Ephesians 4:14 to *"no longer be infants, tossed back and forth by the waves, and blown here and there by every wind of teaching and by the cunning and craftiness of men in their deceitful scheming."*

Ladies, everyone is not going to be healed, everyone is not going to be rich, and everyone is not going to be married. All children won't be obedient and healthy, all financial deals won't go through, every negative circumstance won't pass you by, and God does not exist to do what each of us says He must do for us. We want to hear that we'll be healthy, wealthy, happily married, exempt from difficulty, and able to get God to jump to our every whim. On the other hand, some of us are constantly searching for "the deep things of God." There is nothing deeper than the simple truths set forth in the Bible. Teachers spouting that they have deeper insight or promising you'll have whatever you want are selling you a gross distortion of God's truth. Speakers and preachers who say or even imply such things are the *false* teachers spoken of above.

Consider 2 Timothy 4:3. *"For the time will come when men will not put up with sound doctrine. Instead, to suit their own desires, they will gather around them a great number of teachers to say what their itching ears want to hear."* Does this apply to us? Are we excited to hear the newest spin or are we satisfied getting to know God's character and following His directives? Are we allowing Satan to distract us by listening to false teachers, thereby taking up what they're teaching rather than holding up the shield of faith?

Diversion

The sixth way Satan prevents us from using the shield of faith is by tossing diversions into our paths. In other words, he diverts our beliefs, seducing us to believe in, accept, and spout philosophies other than God's truth. If Satan can coerce us to believe something other than, different from, or askance from God's truth, he's dealt his most lethal blow because we perform that which we truly believe. You see, when we judge any belief system that contradicts the Word of God as solid and sure, Satan has succeeded in totally diverting our attention from the truth. In this state, we have not only lowered the shield, we've put it down and away. At will then, Satan can attack us and we not only have no defense, but we're liable to go down believing God has something to do with our demise.

The mind interprets what we have conditioned it to believe; however, what our senses perceive and what our minds interpret is not always the truth. If our senses and the Word of God contradict, we must conclude that our senses are wrong. God's Word is always the truth and our perceptions must be filtered through the Word.

An overwhelming amount of information in our society purports the message that says promiscuity, homosexuality, ghosts (necromancy), witchcraft, and the like are harmless

POWER SUIT

and acceptable. We make the mistake of forming our opinions about these issues based on what's presented in the media, rather than on what the Word of God has to say about them.

Traci believed abortion was OK. As a 20-year-old college student, she found herself confused, scared, single, and pregnant. Not wanting to disappoint her parents or anyone else who thought she was "different" from other girls who got pregnant and were doomed to hard times, she went to a local pregnancy clinic to confirm what she suspected. With the full support of her boyfriend, she went through with the abortion only to live in the painful grip of that decision for years afterward.

Karen almost believed drug use would be OK. She tells the story this way, "I was so in love with my ex-husband that I chose to ignore signs of impending trouble. I thought he had quit using drugs by the time we were married. I found it was only hidden for awhile. There was a point when I almost walked over to that threshold of drugs. I wanted so much to be a part of him that I was almost willing to do what I knew was wrong and had fought against. It took money being used for drugs instead of bills and physical abuse before I left, and by that time, I was a broken person."

Satan knows how to be subtle.

Sometimes diversions don't seem as serious as the above examples. Satan knows how to be subtle. Another friend, Karen Porter, told me that she'd never watched daytime TV because she always worked full time. When she broke her leg, she was home for months and got interested in a soap opera. When she went back to work and couldn't watch it anymore, she discovered that she could read each day's episode on the Internet. So every day she read what was going on in Brooke, Taylor, Eric, Ridge, and Stephanie's lives. It only took a few minutes; how could it hurt anyone if she simply kept up with the storyline?

Then one day, Karen's pastor said, "Some of you in the audience need to commit to personal holiness." Instant conviction about the soap opera pierced her heart because she realized that every day she was filling her mind and heart with lying, cheating, stealing, affairs, adultery, and such.

Feeding soap-opera style answers and tactics into our minds daily can easily turn into real-life diversions. Surely the enemy of our souls will do his best to engineer circumstances that make us think to solve our problems as the soap opera actresses solve theirs. A best friend's husband starts looking good, lying seems like the easiest way out, and cheating looks like the obvious step to the next level.

Our job is to think on things that are true, honest, just, pure, lovely, and of good report (see Philippians 4:8 KJV); our minds kept on this list will not lead us to divert our attention away from God, but will rather focus our eyes on Him and how He can help us act out these truths.

Second Thessalonians 2:9–10 says, *"The coming of the lawless one will be in accordance with the work of Satan displayed in all kinds of counterfeit miracles, signs and wonders, and in every sort of evil that deceives those who are perishing. They perish because they refused to love the truth and so be saved."*

 Step Aside: What is diverting your attention from God? What have you been seduced to believe is OK? If anything comes to mind, this might be the Holy Spirit nudging you to take a look at those beliefs. Here's what you can do:

1. List the beliefs that come to mind. (For example: maybe you believe abortion is OK; smoking a little marijuana can't hurt; teen boys should be allowed to sow their wild oats; or God accepts your homosexual lifestyle.)

2. Find Scripture passages concerning each of your issues.

3. Write down what Scripture has to say and then check out your findings with a reputable pastor who is true to the teachings of the Bible.

4. What do the following verses say you can do to keep Satan's distractions at bay?
   a. Ephesians 6:11
   b. 1 Peter 5:8–9*a*

A Closing Word

Don't let what you see determine what you believe. Let go of irritations, immoderation, self-absorption, complications, distractions, and diversions. Hold up the shield of faith, no matter what. Faith is not built merely during good, easy times. It's in the face of trouble that God is able to increase our faith. Stand fast against the tricks of Satan and your shield will stand strong for you. Hold your shield and watch from behind it how God works. Once you have faced problems God's way—from behind the shield—you will experience God at work and you'll be stronger to act in faith the next time you face a difficulty. As you experience victories, you will become more and more assured of what the object of your faith is capable of doing on your behalf.

Chapter 6

Crowning

Helmet of Salvation

My son Matthew probably had the shortest football career in history. He went out for the high school squad in the summer before his junior year. During one of the first practices, he received a hit that resulted in a concussion. So ended football for him. I spent the next several months driving him back and forth to the sports medicine clinic for checkups and therapy.

Contrary to the teasing he endured, the problem really had not been Matthew's lack of athleticism. The problem was a poorly fitted helmet. The padding under the helmet was in the wrong place, so when he was hit, the protection the helmet was supposed to provide was compromised and his head took a beating.

American states and the automobile industry understand the importance of protecting the head. We in California have a helmet law requiring that all motorcyclists and their riders wear protective headgear. It's also necessary to wear helmets here when you ride bicycles, in-line skates, and skateboards. In cars, side impact and curtain air bags are being installed to help protect the occupants' heads in the case of an accident. If your head is not protected, you can die.

Just as protection of the physical head can mean life for the physical body, protection of our thoughts can mean life to us emotionally, psychologically, and spiritually. Proverbs 23:7 (KJV) says, *"For as he thinketh in his heart, so is he."* The word for "thinketh" in this verse may be related to a Hebrew word meaning gatekeeper. You see, our thoughts are the gatekeepers of our character. What rattles around up there in our heads is reflective of who we are. If, as the verse says, our thoughts reveal the kind of people we are, then we'd better be extremely careful what we allow ourselves to think if we expect to reflect the image of Christ to a dying world.

So it is that we come to the point of this chapter. The helmets of our Power Suits are not protecting our minds—they are not fitting properly—because of the thought-junk we've allowed to pile up underneath it.

Now notice, the helmet is called the helmet of salvation. The Greek word for *salvation* means deliverance, safety, and health. Let's think this through: this helmet provides us with deliverance, safety, and health by protecting our heads that contain our thoughts, which in turn reflect who we are. So, we cannot accurately reflect who we are in Christ if our thoughts are screwed up, and our thoughts are screwed up without the helmet providing us with deliverance, safety, and health. In other words, wrong thinking adversely affects our liberty, our security, and our energy. Bad character is a result of a corrupted thought life that has happened because the mind has not been covered by the protective helmet of salvation.

So like Matthew's poorly placed padding inside his helmet, what hinders our helmet of salvation from fitting? In essence, I've found the four things that get in the way of our salvation, deliverance, safety, and health/energy are ignorance, doubt, stubbornness, and self-reliance.

Ignorance

No one likes being called ignorant; yet, ignorance is simply the condition of being uneducated, unaware, or uninformed. You're ignorant if you just don't know. If we spend any time pondering that definition, we'll quickly come to understand that two old maxims are far from true: ignorance is *not* bliss, and what you don't know *can indeed* hurt you.

When first used, we didn't know that the force of the suddenly inflated airbag could kill a young child instead of protecting him. For some time, we didn't know cigarette smoking definitely caused cancer. For some time, we didn't know the danger posed by our divided attention while driving and talking on a handheld cell phone. Until these habits caused verifiable, observable problems, we were ignorant of the devastating outcomes.

> Ignorance is simply the condition of being uneducated, unaware, or uninformed.

If Satan, our adversary, can keep us ignorant, we too will experience devastation. Our helmet of salvation won't fit; it won't even be worn. The main thing he would have us blind to is what Christ has supplied us in redemption. Satan is trying to hide from us the way to salvation, which is clearly marked. Jesus Himself tells us, *"I am the way and the truth and the life. No one comes to the Father except through me"* (John 14:6).

We all have sinned, but God has provided a way to escape from the just punishment for that sin and to get straight to Him. The way is belief in what Christ has done for us on the Cross of Calvary, which means not only mental assent, but physical and emotional commitment. That's the plan of salvation. Simple.

Do not allow the enemy of your soul to fool you into thinking that salvation takes more than that; it doesn't. Ephesians 2:8–9 says, *"For it is by grace you have been saved, through faith—and this not from yourselves, it is the gift of God—not by works, so that no one can boast."* Understand that because of God's grace—

His unmerited favor; that which you did not, do not, and cannot deserve—He chooses to see you as righteous through the blood of Jesus Christ. *"God made him [Jesus] who had no sin to be sin for us, so that in him [Jesus] we might become the righteousness of God"* (2 Corinthians 5:21). Being totally ignorant of grace keeps you helmetless, vulnerable, and in danger of missing salvation. Accept the gift. An Old Testament reference makes this clear: *"Turn to me and be saved, all you ends of the earth; for I am God, and there is no other"* (Isaiah 45:22).

Once saved, though, even with the helmet on, it may not be fitting snugly. Salvation is an eternal issue and the helmet protects us from damnation in hell, but it's also a day-to-day, continual process born out through deliverance, safety, and health. Do not be ignorant of any of these. Vigilance involves realizing we could still have a problem if we don't tighten down these "straps."

Do not be ignorant of the deliverance God provides

"Be self-controlled and alert. Your enemy the devil prowls around like a roaring lion looking for someone to devour" (1 Peter 5:8). Satan ensnares us by patiently drawing us into his traps. As I've heard it said: toeholds become footholds, and footholds become strongholds. Something a little askew seems harmless so we participate. When we're not immediately negatively affected, we repeat the behavior. Before long, our involvement is habitual. Voilà, we are in bondage, only able to extricate ourselves with an incredible amount of tenacity, resolve, and prayer.

My friend Chelsea,* one of the strongest Christian women I know on the planet, found herself caught up in astrology. Her popular high school English teacher talked so excitedly about the discipline that Chelsea's interest piqued. Toehold. The teacher drew her into the discipline by instructing her to do her own astrological chart. Foothold. Then Chelsea delved even deeper into the practice by preparing other people's charts. Stronghold. Thankfully, once she was no longer in that teacher's class and as her commitment to the Lord grew, she felt compelled to drop astrology, but even then, it was difficult to break the habit.

Look to God for deliverance from the toeholds, footholds, and strongholds in your own life. Whether you've been drawn in by dabbling with alcohol as a social drinker, addiction to prescription drugs, overspending, overeating, or choosing the wrong kind of men, God can deliver you.

The promise of God's deliverance from any level of bondage is nowhere more simply stated than in John 8:36, *"So if the Son sets you free, you will be free indeed."* The Greek word *free* used here signifies to liberate from moral, ceremonial, or mortal liability; to deliver. God liberates us, frees us, and releases us from liability when He breaks the strongholds in our lives. To be ignorant of this truth is like refusing to walk out of an unlocked prison cell. We remove the hindrance of bondage from under the helmet of salvation when we choose to walk in the deliverance God provides.

 Step Aside: According to the following verses, beside Satan, what else helps to entrap us?

PSALM 9:16 *The LORD is known by his justice; the wicked are ensnared by the work of their hands.*

PROVERBS 18:7 *A fool's mouth is his undoing, and his lips are a snare to his soul.*

PROVERBS 12:13 *An evil man is trapped by his sinful talk, but a righteous man escapes trouble.*

2 THESSALONIANS 2:9–10 *The coming of the lawless one will be in accordance with the work of Satan displayed in all kinds of counterfeit miracles, signs and wonders, and in every sort of evil*

that deceives those who are perishing. They perish because they refused to love the truth and so be saved.

Do Not Be ignorant of the Safety God Supplies

Throughout the Bible, we read incidents over and over again of God's protective love for His children. God protected Noah, his family, and the land animals during the cataclysmic flood that wiped out all other life on earth. God protected the infant Moses in the little basket his mother prepared for him during his Nile River cruise, taking him directly to Pharaoh's palace where he was then adopted and raised as a prince. God protected David throughout Saul's murderous rampages. God protected the infant Jesus, first keeping Mary His mother from the societal implications of her unplanned pregnancy, and then moving Him to Egypt to escape the genocidal tirade of King Herod. The New Testament finds Christ calming a sea that was threatening to sink the disciples' boat, and rescuing Peter from drowning during his water-walking incident.

Assurance of safety or security is always a function on my knowledge of who I am, whose I am, and what resources are available to me. John's comments in 1 John 4:4 make this clear: *"You, dear children, are from God and have overcome them, because the one who is in you is greater than the one who is in the world."* Who am I? I am an overcomer. Whose am I? I am God's. What resources are available to me? All the power of the One who is greater than the power in the world.

When I got married, I took on a new identity. I am now a wife, but not just any wife; I'm James Elliott's wife. I know who I am and whose I am. But more than that, I became aware of resources available to me, which are all the resources of the man who married me. I am secure in the resources supplied and managed by my husband in our household.

In a greater way, we can all depend on God for security. When problems rear their ugly heads, we can rest securely in Him. He provides spiritual, emotional, physical, and mental security. When issues in any area threaten to undo us, we must remember that we're secure in Christ from all danger. God is more than capable of coming to our rescue. Being secure is an expression of faith; faith dispels fear that is brought on by danger. Knowing who you are in God allows you to be secure and to exercise your faith to kick fear out from under your helmet.

 Step Aside: Read the following verses and write God a prayer of thanksgiving for safety and security as you see them expressed here:

1 JOHN 5:4 *For everyone born of God overcomes the world. This is the victory that has overcome the world, even our faith.*

JOHN 16:33 *I have told you these things, so that in me you may have peace. In this world you will have trouble. But take heart! I have overcome the world.*

Do not be ignorant of the health (energy) God assigns

God has always been concerned about our health and vitality. In the Law, He gave the Hebrew people regulations about their diet, prohibiting animals such as pigs and rabbits that were especially prone to infections with parasites. The rituals they observed helped them maintain sanitary conditions. "The strict laws about sexual morality among the Hebrew people also promoted the prevention of venereal disease. Circumcision of males was not only a religious rite, but also a hygienic measure that reduced infection and cancer," according to *Nelson's Illustrated Bible Dictionary.*

Even a cursory reading of the Gospels proves that God continued His concern about disease and death. Follow Christ through the Scriptures and we see that sickness couldn't hang around in His presence and we never witness Jesus attending a funeral. In fact, the two times we see Him near dead people, He raised them. (See Luke 7:11–15 and John 11:41–43.)

Jesus saves, Jesus delivers, Jesus provides security, and Jesus also heals. What is healing? Healing is release from disease. Look at the word *disease*. It's actually made up of two parts. The prefix, *dis*, means without or away. The root, *ease*, means freedom from labor, pain, or physical annoyance; tranquil rest; comfort. So when I experience disease, I am experiencing a separation from rest and comfort. To be healed then is to be restored to a place of rest. This can happen suddenly, as in the case of the many miraculous healings we read in the Bible, or it can happen gradually, in our outlook, and even in death.

We may have been healed many times that we don't know of. Germs and viruses seeking to attack our bodies may have been warded off with more than the natural defenses God so graciously gave us in our immune system. We could have been exposed to some killer infection that God just said no to without even alerting us or our physicians, but I know for sure of one time when I experienced a miraculous, immediate healing.

I was a student at Biola University and just as our annual Torrey Bible Conference began, I started coming down with my annual case of strep throat. After attending the opening keynote session and hearing Dr. Bruce Wilkinson's inspiring message, I went to a piano in one of the music building's practice rooms and wrote a praise song highlighting the conference's theme, Lord, What Would You Have Me to Do?

That evening, I gathered my dorm friends together and sang the song for them, but I noticed my throat was getting scratchy. They loved the song, but we really thought no more about it as the week progressed and we got deeper into the conference sessions. My throat grew worse as the days passed and I didn't get antibiotics until the week was almost over. By then, my voice was completely gone, I couldn't speak at all much less sing, and it was torture to swallow.

Still I refused to miss the closing session. After Dr. Wilkinson's closing message, he asked if anyone would like to come to the microphone to express comments and testimonies about the week. As my dorm friends and I sat in the full gymnasium, they leaned over to me and said I should go up and share the song. I turned to them, pointed to my throat, and fully expected to only mouth my answer, but out came, "But I can't even talk," as clear as day. I was shocked. I swallowed; no pain. I blinked and swallowed again; no pain at all. The strep throat was completely gone!

Some healings— restorations of energy—take time.

I wasn't a public speaker at the time, so it was pretty daunting to walk all the way to the front of that gym and not only share the testimony of what had just happened to me, but to then go to the grand piano and play and sing the song. I ended up teaching the simple chorus to everyone in that huge auditorium.

Lord, what would you have me to do?
I want only to follow You.
With my eyes on Your Son,
I've only begun
The great journey that you'll carry me through.
©1979 Sharon Norris

I was restored back to health that day, and in 30 years, have never been stricken with strep throat again. I haven't been healed that way of every sickness I've ever experienced, but of that healing, I am sure.

Some healings—restorations of energy—take time. The common cold usually runs its course. Sometimes God uses a doctor's intervention and at other times, God gives us grace to endure lingering ailments such as lupus, diabetes, asthma, etc. I'm not saying Jesus can't or won't heal even those problems, but can't you see how having the illness in our bodies yet moving on in victorious living in spite of it is also release from disease?

Even death is a healing for the Christian. We understand heaven to consist of no more sorrow or sickness. Before my godly parents died, they were suffering from illnesses that caused their bodies to fail, but that dropped away once their spirits joined with God in Glory. That's got to be the best healing of all.

 Step Aside: In light of our previous discussion, restate the truths of the following verses as if you were going to explain them to your friends.

JAMES 5:14–16 *Is any one of you sick? He should call the elders of the church to pray over him and anoint him with oil in the name of the Lord. And the prayer offered in faith will make the sick person well; the Lord will raise him up. If he has sinned, he will be forgiven. Therefore confess your sins to each other and pray for each other so that you may be healed. The prayer of a righteous man is powerful and effective.*

1 CORINTHIANS 15:55–57 *"Where, O death, is your victory? Where, O death, is your sting?" The sting of death is sin, and the power of sin is the law. But thanks be to God! He gives us the victory through our Lord Jesus Christ.*

Banish ignorance with knowledge and you'll short-circuit the ability of ignorance to keep your Power Suit helmet from fitting properly. Avail yourself of the wealth of Scriptures that teach you all about salvation, deliverance, safety, and health. Perhaps you might try designing a Bible study regimen to immerse yourself in the knowledge of the truth about each of those four elements. For each element, assign yourself a specific amount of time to search the Scriptures on the topic. Write down and study those verses. Maybe memorize a few. Then read a book on the subject written by a solid, biblical expositor. (Ask your pastor for a recommendation.)

Doubt

Like ignorance, doubt also gets in the way of our salvation, deliverance, safety and health. When we doubt, we are uncertain or undecided in our opinion or in our belief. Since doubt is a function of our thought life, the uncertainty and indecision produced by it makes our helmets loose and thus allows our heads to be targets for those flaming arrows Satan likes to hurl our way.

Consider JAMES 1:5–8:
If any of you lacks wisdom, he should ask God, who gives generously to all without finding fault, and it will be given to him. But when he asks, he must believe and not doubt, because he who doubts is like a wave of the sea, blown and tossed by the wind. That man should not think he will receive anything from the Lord; he is a double-minded man, unstable in all he does.

In the above verse, God lets us know there is absolutely no need for doubt in our lives. When we're unsure of anything, we can ask God and He will generously give us the wisdom we need to make the right decision. That should be the end of the doubt.

Once we check with God and make any necessary adjustments, it's time to let doubt go and move on.

Doubt does, however, have a purpose to serve. It should make us pause long enough to think things through. Then once we check with God and make any necessary adjustments, it's time to let doubt go and move on. When we check in, if God says continue toward the destination, then do so. If He says alter the course, then we alter it. The point is we don't stop living altogether because we've experienced a moment of doubt. Doubt provides the check and balance we need to keep us from running amok, but we do continue to live and move. Doubt was never intended to be a permanent address. Living on Doubt Street makes us sitting ducks for Satan's attacks because while we're lingering, we're not fulfilling our God-ordained purpose.

I believe two main things cause us to move into a residence on Doubt Street. First is impatience. We stick with doubt when we deem that it takes too much time to get the answer we want. After a while, we wonder whether we were right to think whatever we thought in the first place. "Was that really God's voice?" we ask. "Maybe that was a stupid idea in the first place," we ponder. James 1:4 says, *"But let patience have her perfect work, that ye may be perfect and entire, wanting nothing."* When impatience is causing doubt, it's time to cool your jets. Stop and let patience work some maturity and completeness into your life. And consider this: God could be saying, "No."

The second cause of doubt is insecurity. We say and think things like, "I'm not good enough"; or "I don't think I'll ever be able to…;" and "That just must not have been for me." As long as we believe we can't, we won't. We only take strides toward that which we believe we can accomplish.

My niece Meloni shared with me her struggle with doubt:

> *My dream is to sing around the world and minister in an effort to bring souls to Christ. I should be traveling, teaching, and preaching through song and doing God's work. I've been given the gift, so why not use it? Why? Because I doubt that my voice is good enough; because I feel my physical appearance is not pleasing to the eye; because I'm not strong enough in the Word to witness to others and save souls; because I am afraid of rejection and I totally doubt that I would be heard.*

I know Meloni. She has a heart to serve God and a beautiful voice. Her reservations are all the product of prolonged doubt that will hinder her from changing the things she can change and learning to live with the things she can't. God's call is the important thing. If God has called Meloni to minister through song, then He's also equipped her to do so. That takes the voice and strength issues off of the table. Acceptance or rejection is none of her concern either if God has called her, so that takes the rejection and appearance issues out of play as well. What's left? Not one excuse. Meloni, get busy with your ministry in song.

Meloni's doubts may mean for her to enhance her voice through professional lessons, enlist the assistance of an image consultant for new direction on hair, wardrobe, and makeup, or maybe join a gym or hire a personal trainer. These ideas will strengthen her outer image while she moves away from Doubt Street and gets on with her ministry so people can be blessed.

Take off the doubt so your helmet will fit. Satan wants to keep you in doubt so you won't step out.

 Step Aside: Doubt is keeping Meloni bound; it's hindering her from being delivered into her ministry. Answer the following questions regarding your relationship to doubt:

Is doubt stopping you from being delivered into your ministry? Or perhaps it's obstructing your deliverance from a destructive situation. There is somewhere else you can go; someone else who cares for you.

Is doubt hindering your salvation because you are thinking you're not good enough for God to save you? You're right, and you'll never be good enough. God saves sinners, not good people.

Are you allowing doubt to hamper your safety and damage your health? Do you doubt your ability to maintain a loving relationship so you self-destruct by overeating, overspending, and becoming a workaholic?

Stubbornness

The third hindrance to our salvation, deliverance, safety, and health is stubbornness. My friend Lillian told me a very illustrative story about her own stubbornness. The drum beat of ambition and the thought of fulfilling a lifelong dream to renovate an old farmhouse tuned out her sister's words of caution, "Are you sure you are up to living here? It gets really cold and that's a lot of grass to mow. Perhaps you should think twice about taking on a big house. You really should consider moving to a warmer climate and to a place that requires less work."

If God was speaking, Lillian was not listening. She tuned both Him and her sister out. Besides, Lillian had a reputation for being a maverick. Determined to blaze her own trail, she moved into her dream house three years ago; of senior age and single. Soon after, oil prices shot up, renovation overruns stretched her budget, and auto repair costs added to unexpected budget shortfalls. And, over time, she got sick and tired of snow! To say she regretted not listening and settling in a warmer climate is a gross understatement. Memories of her mother's words took up where her sister's voice left off, *"A hard head makes a sore back."*

Lillian's brand of stubbornness is nothing new. Luckily, her decision didn't have eternal consequences, but we can exercise this same kind of obstinacy on issues that will block the perfect fit of the Power Suit helmet. When my Sunday School class studied the Book of Romans, many students were amazed at the moxie of those discussed in chapter one. Here were people who boldly made a decision against God. They decided not to retain God in their knowledge so their hearts were hardened and they became fools, given over to degrading passions so that they would eventually destroy themselves.

God has given us all the answers we need and a clear picture of Himself. If we stubbornly refuse to believe, we successfully hinder the protection of the helmet of the Power Suit. Satan can fire off a dart of any ungodly thought and we'll run with it.

If we refuse to believe in the redemptive Word and work

of Jesus Christ, we've been hit by a fiery dart and will miss heaven.

If we refuse to accept God's way of deliverance, we've been hit by a fiery dart and will remain bound.

If we reject God's model for safety in relationships (as single and celibate, or in marriage between a man and a woman) and in child-rearing (disciplining children while they are young), we've been stung by a fiery dart and will suffer from the fallout years later.

If we stubbornly refuse to eat right and take care of our bodies—the temple of God—we've been hit be a fiery dart and will suffer physically and emotionally.

Step Aside: In what ways are you stubbornly refusing your salvation, deliverance, safety, or health?

Self-Reliance

The fourth hindrance to our salvation, deliverance, safety, and health is self-reliance. The Bible never even hints at an intention for us to travel through life keeping a stiff upper lip and braving it on our own. God desires for us to be dependent on Him. But boy oh boy, we have a grand time from our earliest ages, belligerently insisting, "I can do it myself!" This attitude, inbred in us thanks to the sin nature, keeps our Power Suit helmet from fitting because our thoughts are riveted on our own selfish desires rather than on God's desires for us. And when we shut out what God wants in favor of getting what we want, trouble always follows.

Abraham, the father of the faithful, and his wife Sarah made this drastic mistake. We can read the whole sordid story in Genesis 16–25, but the upshot is they wanted a child, God promised them a child, but it took too long in their eyes for them to get pregnant, so Sarah took matters into her own hands. She relied upon a societal rule of the day to get her baby. So Sarah gave her handmaiden, Hagar, to her husband to be his second wife. Any child Hagar would bear would be Sarah's legal property.

And so the plan played itself out—at least until Sarah got fed up with Hagar. Abraham and God had to intervene to keep Sarah from banishing Hagar to the wilderness. Finally, Hagar had Ishmael and Sarah claimed the baby as her own son. Fourteen years passed and God stepped back into their drama, allowing Sarah to get pregnant with Isaac, the promised son. It didn't take long before Sarah found another excuse to banish Hagar and Ishmael, the baby she had wanted and raised as her own. That's cold-blooded, but that's not all. We can thank Sarah and Abraham for the Middle East crisis today because the opposing sides are descendants of Ishmael and Isaac.

And so the plan played itself out—at least until Sarah got fed up with Hagar.

Sarah and Abraham relied upon themselves rather than relying on God and they really made a mess of things. Do we do this same kind of thing today? Of course we do. My friend Bonita* shared a modern-day incident with me that could have caused havoc in her family because she was relying on her own judgment. Here's Bonita's story:

> When our son moved back in, my husband gave him two weeks to get a job or he would have to leave home, again. Since it usually takes our son months and months to get a job, I worried. A few days before "kick-out day," I felt frightened about our decision. If he didn't find a job, I pictured our son on the street, sleeping by the curb, lost, alone, and angry. How would that help him? Who would hire an unshowered, unshaven, homeless person? How can you expect a mother to kick out her own flesh and blood?
>
> Telling my husband I felt uncomfortable about our decision caused a lot of stress between us. In the end,

I supported him but cringed inside and told the Lord, OK, God. I'll do this, but You sure expect a lot out of me!

The next day, my son bounded in the kitchen door. "Mom! You've got to pray for me! I might have a job! I just have to update my résumé," he said sitting down at the computer. "How do you spell _____? Is the printer working? I have to hurry.... I told him I'd be right back! The job is only a few blocks away. I can even walk there."

After a few minutes he ran out the door. Later he came back and had the biggest smile on his face. "I got a job and I start the day after tomorrow!"

As I look back, I see things clearly. I didn't need to worry and stress my husband out by trying to change our plan. I didn't need to step in to manipulate events to protect my son. God had the bases covered. And I suppose that if our son was kicked out to the street, God would have had that base covered too.

The August 4 entry of Chambers' *My Utmost for His Highest* devotion says, "As long as you think there is something in you, He (God) cannot choose you because you have ends of your own to serve." When we are self-reliant instead of God-reliant, we adopt a works-for-salvation mentality. We hamper God's ability to get through to us because we're so busy telling ourselves what we should do. You can see then how self-reliance can effectively keep us from salvation (I don't need God), deliverance (I can extricate myself), safety (that warning doesn't apply to me), and health (I'm eating, drinking, smoking, etc., whatever I want). Self-reliance on; helmet off or pretty darn loose.

 Step Aside: To close this chapter, rewrite the verses that follow in first person, making each one your own statement against self-reliance.

PROVERBS 3:5 *Trust in the LORD with all your heart and lean not on your own understanding.*

Example:
I will check in with God and be determined to do what He says about every situation rather than depend solely upon what I think I should do.

PROVERBS 3:7 *Do not be wise in your own eyes; fear the LORD and shun evil.*

PROVERBS 28:26 *He who trusts in himself is a fool, but he who walks in wisdom is kept safe.*

JEREMIAH 9:23–24 *This is what the LORD says: "Let not the wise man boast of his wisdom or the strong man boast of his strength or the rich man boast of his riches, but let him who boasts boast about this: that he understands and knows me, that I am the LORD, who exercises kindness, justice and righteousness on earth, for in these I delight," declares the LORD.*

ISAIAH 12:2 *Surely God is my salvation; I will trust and not be afraid. The LORD, the LORD, is my strength and my song; he has become my salvation."*

JEREMIAH 17:7–8 *But blessed is the man who trusts in the LORD, whose confidence is in him. He will be like a tree planted by the water that sends out its roots by the stream. It does not fear when heat comes; its leaves are always green. It has no worries in a year of drought and never fails to bear fruit.*

MATTHEW 11:28–30 *"Come to me, all you who are weary and burdened, and I will give you rest. Take my yoke upon you and learn from me, for I am gentle and humble in heart, and you will find rest for your souls. For my yoke is easy and my burden is light."*

POWER SUIT

Section 4

God's Word, Prayer, and Witnessing

Chapter 7

Just the Right Accessory

The Sword of the Spirit, the Word of God

No outfit is complete without the proper accessories. And ladies, we know how to do it, don't we? Perfect jewelry, a silk scarf, a lapel pin, a fancy belt, and just the right handbag dress up even the simplest ensemble. Well, since we've covered all the articles of clothing associated with the Power Suit, it's now time to accessorize. We won't be decorated with lots of bling because the suit we're wearing is for the purpose of warfare; however, any feminine warrior with good fighting-fashion sense knows that the necessary accessory for this outfit is the right weapon. Getting all dressed up means nothing unless we're properly strapped—that means we're carrying the weapon essential for the fight.

I asked my brother Nick, the retired USMC captain I spoke of earlier in this book, how marines are trained to use and know their weapons. He told me.

"Every marine, whether officer or enlisted man, is a rifleman. The sole purpose of boot camp and Officer Candidate School (OCS) is to train the individual marine in the basic skills of combat survival. No matter what the occupational specialty, every marine is an 0300, a basic infantryman, therefore making him the most lethal weapon on the face of the earth."

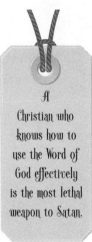

A Christian who knows how to use the Word of God effectively is the most lethal weapon to Satan.

"To maintain that reputation," Nick continued, "the individual marine must master every in and out of his basic weapon. When using the M-14 rifle, every marine knows to "pull" (the operating rod to the rear to clear the chamber), "push" (the operating rod forward to chamber the round), "tap" (the magazine from the bottom to check that it's fully ceded), and "aim and fire" (all done in a fraction of a second). Each infantry rifleman must be able to partially and/or completely field strip his weapon and reassemble it in the dark, being confident that it's done correctly because he and his fellow Marine riflemen are depending on their weapons to stay alive on the battlefield."

What a perfect analogy. A Christian who knows how to use the Word of God effectively is the most lethal weapon to Satan on the face of the earth. Satan and his demons quake in fear before Jesus who is the living Word of God. (See John 1:1, 14, and James 2:19.) When we are in our full Power Suit, Satan can't tell us from Christ until we open our mouths and start to talk crazy. When dealing with the enemy, we should sound like Jesus did when Satan tempted Him and out of our mouths should come, "It is written."

We are that lethal weapon when we "pull" sin from our lives by accepting Christ's forgiving work He finished at Calvary, "push" the Word of God into ourselves daily, "tap" into the mind of Christ by allowing the Holy Spirit to direct us as to exactly how to use the Word, and then "aim and fire" accurately, applying the Word with wisdom, reverence, love, and respect.

With all the other pieces of the armor, we have discussed how they may not fit because of the other junk we haven't yet taken off. In the case of our weaponry, that which gets in the way of the Word of God is our inability to use it properly. Marines would flunk out of boot camp and OCS if they didn't know and couldn't use their weapon. We'll experience the same fate and flunk out as effective Christian witnesses if we don't know and can't use our weapon—God's Word.

The Reason to Study God's Word

Second Timothy 2:15 says, *"Do your best to present yourself to God as one approved, a workman who does not need to be ashamed and who **correctly handles the word of truth**"* (emphasis added). The words *do your best* in the above verse are translated "study" in the King James Version and are derived from the Greek word *spoudazo*, which means to use speed, to make effort, be prompt or earnest, give diligence, and labor. To show yourself as one approved means that you are acceptable because you have been tried or tested. You are a workman who has toiled in order to pass the truth along to others accurately.

If we want to be good at anything, we must spend time with it. From the age of 5 until I was 16, I took classical piano lessons. Every Thursday, I sat at a piano in Mrs. Dolly Perry's backyard room as she and my John Thompson books taught me to play. Halfway through the levels of those red books, Mrs. Perry added studies from *Hanon the Virtuoso Pianist*. My fingers ran up and down the keyboard playing scales and performing exercises. At home, I'd practice a half-hour every day. By the time I entered high school and stopped taking lessons, I could read any piece of music; perform the works of the masters like Bach, Beethoven, and Chopin; and accompany my church's children's choir. I eventually progressed to composing my own praise choruses and leading the praise and worship time at church.

Building bit by bit over those 11 years made me skillful on the piano. Studying God's Word makes us skillful in its use; to reach a decent level of proficiency takes the same kind of diligence as my years at the piano.

The Reality of Studying God's Word

"All right," you say. "I understand that the Bible is God's Word and God's Word is my sword, the number one weapon I can use against Satan, my enemy, in the spiritual warfare I'm in. I'm convinced that I need to study my Bible so I can properly use it as a weapon. But how?"

Great question. Let's look at practical ways to become familiar with the Word of God. These pointers assist us in planning for Bible study. We'll hang our pointers on the acronym WORD. In order to use God's Word effectively, we must:

> **W**ork at studying the Word
> **O**bey the Word
> **R**ehearse the Word
> **D**iscuss the Word

W—Work at Studying the Word

A good workman knows his tools, a great pianist knows her keyboard, a skilled marine knows his weapon, and an effective Christian warrior knows the Word of God. Obtaining this knowledge takes lots of work. To study God's Word effectively, besides our willingness, we need three other things: supplies, a schedule, and a system.

Supplies: In order to make your study time the most beneficial, the first and most important supply you'll need is a good study Bible, one that's accurate, understandable, and helpful. When judging accuracy, choose a translation rather than a paraphrase from which to study. A translation can be a word-for-word type or a thought-for-thought type; either kind will give you a legitimate reading of what was said in the original languages. (A paraphrase involves a freer wording from the original text, and is not best for beginners' firsthand study of the Bible.)

For understandability, there are many versions of good translations from which to choose. I grew up using the King

James Version (abbreviated KJV) and have memorized many verses from it, so that's the version I like to use most. However, because people get hung up on the Old English vocabulary of the KJV, the New King James Version (NKJV) has been introduced. It is very much like the KJV but with updated changes like replacing "thee" and "thou" for the more commonly used "you" and "your." Other popular translations are the New International Version (NIV), the New American Standard Bible (NASB), and the New Living Translation (NLT).

As far as study helps within the Bible are concerned, look for notations that will lead you to cross-references. These are verses in other parts of the Bible that are associated in some way to the verse you are reading. Cross-references are usually listed down the center of the pages or at the ends of the verses. It would also be nice if your Bible included a concordance which is a compilation of names and key words found in Scripture. Use a concordance to locate verses you want to find that contain particular words of interest to you. Lots of Bibles also include maps of biblical lands so when a location is mentioned in the Scriptures, you can look it up on the map and get an idea of where the people were at the time. The study Bible I use, the *Key Word Study Bible*, KJV (AMG Publishers), contains all of the above items plus lexical aids (extended definitions from the Hebrew and Greek words), grammatical codes, introductions to each book, footnotes, and Strong's concise Hebrew and Greek dictionaries.

A computer software program will assist your navigation through the Bible.

Other supplies that will help you study your Bible are a notebook, a pen, highlighters, and a computer software program. Use the notebook and pen to jot down your personal insights from your study times, and use the highlighters to mark verses that are special to you. A computer software program will assist your navigation through the Bible as it will allow you to quickly find cross-references, look up definitions, compare different Bible versions, and more. Software programs can be purchased online or at your local Christian bookstore, or some free internet sites like BibleGateway.com, Bible.org, and BlueLetterBible.org allow you to use some of the tools included in purchased programs.

 Step Aside: Go into a Bible bookstore; lay different translations side by side; and compare passages like 1 Corinthians 13, Ephesians 6, and Psalms 1 and 23. Purchase the translation that's most understandable for you.

Schedule: Once you have gathered all your supplies, it's going to be necessary for you to schedule Bible study into your days. It has been said, "If you fail to plan, you plan to fail." You will not be successful at Bible study if you do not plan to do it. Your busy life and your adversary, the devil, will make sure you fail if you are not disciplined at it. In order to fit Bible study into my day, I've found it necessary to prioritize, deputize, and organize.

You must decide that studying the Bible is a priority. Attach your Bible study or devotional time to some other habit you already do. I have made my devotional time a part of my morning ritual: get out of bed, use the bathroom, brush my teeth, read my Bible and pray as I spend my time on the treadmill, write my daily devotion, take my shower, apply my makeup, get dressed, drink my orange juice, take my vitamins, eat breakfast, get to work. (OK, so I don't always eat breakfast like I should. You caught me.) For me, if I don't get the reading and prayer done in the morning, it probably won't happen later on during the day. On Saturdays and vacation days I can allocate a longer time. Then if I want or need to do additional study, I can do so in the evenings.

Other prioritizing ideas include disciplining yourself not to answer your email every day, refusing to eat dinner, or not going to bed until you have read your Bible. To remind yourself of each of the above commitments, place your Bible in front of your computer screen, on the dining room table, or on your pillow.

Since you can't suddenly become twins, you're going to have to stop doing something in order to find the time to study your Bible. Think about how you can deputize. What are some things you are doing that others around you can do? For example, if you're a homemaker with children, what can the children do for you? If you drive to work alone daily, perhaps you can find someone else to drive with you. Carpool, and on the mornings when it's not your turn to drive, read on the way to work.

Finally, if you are going to stick successfully to a schedule, you must organize. Many of us live by our daily planners, calendars, and cell phones. If that's you, write down or type in your Bible study commitment. Be creative and build flexibility into your plan. Maybe you'll do better starting with a three- or four-day per week plan. If you cook dinner every night, why not spend Monday evening cooking five meals? Eat one meal on Monday, then use the cooking time you save on Tuesday through Friday to study your Bible. Purchase the Bible on tape and listen to your reading as you drive the freeways to and from work or as you do the housework. Study your Bible as you wait for your kids to finish soccer practice. The time is there, you just have to find it. The possibilities are endless.

 Step Aside: Use the Scheduling Work Sheet on page 166 to get a clear picture of how you spend your time. Follow the directions on page 167 to get you started on your personal Bible study schedule.

SCHEDULING WORK SHEET

	SUN	MON	TUES	WED	THURS	FRI	SAT
5:00 A.M.							
6:00							
7:00							
8:00							
9:00							
10:00							
11:00							
12:00 P.M.							
1:00							
2:00							
3:00							
4:00							
5:00							
6:00							
7:00							
8:00							
9:00							
10:00							
11:00							
12:00 A.M.							
1:00							
2:00							
3:00							
4:00							

Directions:

1. Use a pencil with a good eraser.

2. Draw lines, arrows, or Xs through the hours of each day which are occupied by employment, ministry, or other regular activities. (For example, if you work 9:00 A.M.– 5:00 P.M., Monday to Friday, draw a line through all those hours because you cannot be otherwise occupied.)

Write in the names of the activities.

Cross out travel time and sleep time.

Schedule time for the following:

> Quiet time with the Lord
> Private time with spouse
> Private time with children
> Relaxation with friends
> Personal exercise

NOTE: You may now make use of your eraser. What activities can you "deputize," or what activities can you reorganize or multitask so you won't have to spend so much time on them? Rearrange your activities and schedule in your Bible study. Make a note to inform the person to whom you will delegate any responsibilities.

Systems: The idea of Bible study is to get something out of the Scriptures every time you read them. Keep in mind that our goal is to get to know the Word of God well enough to be able to use it effectively against Satan's fiery-dart attacks. Understanding this, we don't just approach the Bible haphazardly. In order to go into Bible study purposefully, adopt an organized system of study. Here are some study methods to get you started.

The Inductive Method: Use this method to extract the meaning out of any verse or passage of Scripture. Read the selection and then ask and answer three questions: What does it say? What does it mean? What does it mean for me?

For example, consider James 1:5, *"If any of you lacks wisdom, he should ask God, who gives generously to all without finding fault, and it will be given to him."* What does it say? The verse says that the person who does not have wisdom can ask for wisdom from God and God will generously give it to him. What does that mean? According to *Nelson's Illustrated Bible Dictionary*, wisdom is the "ability to judge correctly and to follow the best course of action, based on knowledge and understanding." And according to the *New Unger's Bible Dictionary*, "Wisdom is in the deepest sense a divine gift." So, this verse means that God will give a person who asks for it the ability to judge a situation correctly and the divine knowledge to follow the best course of action.

Now personalize this: What does it mean for me? This verse is telling me that whenever I'm not sure of what to do in a situation and I don't know which choice I should make, I can ask God and be assured that He will let me know the exact right thing to do. (Not necessarily instantaneously.)

Read and Summarize: Another method of study is to read a passage and then summarize what you've just read. I recently used this method when I reread the Minor Prophets (Hosea through Malachi). Not having read these books in some time, I wanted a general overview of what each book was about. Every morning, I read one chapter and then used a spiral notebook to write out what that chapter had been about. By the time I had read all the books, I had my own personal commentary completed.

Word or Theme Study: You will enjoy a study of specific words or themes in the Bible. Go through the Scriptures and find out what God has to say about love, justice, forgiveness, grace, mercy, laughter, life, power, or patience. Choose any topic. By doing this, you will develop the mind of Christ on each issue and come away knowing how to think as He does about it.

Character Study: I love people, so one of my favorite ways to study Scripture is by getting to know the biblical characters. For this method, put yourself in the shoes of the people in the Bible story. I developed a new appreciation for the one leper out of ten who turned back to thank Jesus for healing him (Luke 17:11–19). By becoming this guy in my imagination, I first realized that I was a Samaritan. I hated the Jews and they hated me. I had to be pretty bad off to even ask this Jewish guy (Jesus) for help in the first place. Then to have this Jew actually help me—oh my goodness—no wonder I had to turn back, give up my prejudices, and worship Him. Through this study, I also learned that Jesus intends for me to give up my prejudices to worship Him.

 Step Aside: Practice using each of the following study methods.

WEEK ONE: Use the inductive method. Each day, choose a verse of Scripture. Write that Scripture on the top of a sheet of paper and write each question, spaced out, down the side of the sheet. Now answer each question pertaining to the verse you chose.

WEEK TWO: Study the Book of Ruth. It only has four chapters. Read and summarize a chapter each day, Monday through Thursday. On Friday, write a reflection of what the message of the book meant to you and what you hear God indicating to you through it.

WEEK THREE: Choose a Bible story and put yourself in the shoes of each character. Become each person in your imagination as you read the story. For example, if you choose the story of the woman with the issue of blood in Luke 8:43–48, read it through once as the woman, read it again seeing the incident through Peter's eyes, and then read it again looking at it from Jesus' perspective.

O — Obey the Word

Good soldiers abide by what they learn. What good is it to get all dressed up in the Power Suit and know all about warfare and weapons and then refuse to use them when the fight starts? An effective Christian warrior has an attitude to submit to what the Bible says. This takes vulnerability to let the Word change us. Our determination should be that whatever the Bible says, we will believe and obey.

This gets down to the nitty-gritty. For example, Exodus 20:15 says, *"You shall not steal,"* therefore, not only will we pay for the things we want from stores, but we also will not buy or watch bootleg videos. This includes burning copies of CDs and making photocopies of copyrighted material. And despite the current fashion trend, Leviticus 19:28 says, *"Do not cut your bodies for the dead or put tattoo marks on yourselves. I am the LORD,"* so staying out of the tattoo parlor is an easy decision for us.

If we intend for our weapon to work for us, we have to operate it properly or it's liable to blow up in our faces. The same book that promises the blessings of obedience promises curses upon disobedience. We cannot ignore the latter or think those verses don't apply to us because we're sincere. We will find ourselves sincerely wrong and punished for our noncompliance. James 4:7–8 is clear: *"Submit (put yourself under in obedience in subjection) yourselves, then, to God. Resist the devil, and he will flee from you. Come near (approach: get close) to God and he will come near to you. Wash your hands, you sinners, and purify your hearts, you double-minded"* (parenthetical statements mine).

R — Rehearse the Word

During my late teens and early 20s, I got pretty good at memorizing Scripture. The other members of my semiprofessional gospel group and I would play "Hit You with the Word" whenever we had some free time during rehearsals or while traveling. One person would begin by calling another's name and then recite from memory a Scripture and its reference. That person would then have to quote a different Scripture and reference in response. We would continue "hitting" each other back and forth until one person couldn't think of a Scripture to recite. Then the game would either be over, or another person would jump into the "fight." No one ever liked to lose.

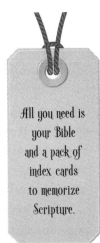

All you need is your Bible and a pack of index cards to memorize Scripture.

OK, I know you're either thinking, *You were a weird teenager*, or *I can't do it. I was never good at memorizing*. Not so on either count. You can do it. In fact, I'm going to give you a great method that I used to memorize Scripture and I rarely lost the "Hit You" game. All you need is your Bible and a pack of index cards.

Step One: Start with one index card and label it "Daily." On this card, write only the Scripture reference for a verse you wish to memorize. Carry this card with you every day (thus the name "Daily" card). Whenever you get a chance, look at this card and open your Bible to the verse. Repeat the verse until you can look at the reference and say the verse without having to look it up.

Step Two: Now label a set of cards for each day of the week, from Monday through Saturday. Once you can say the verse on the "Daily" card by just looking at the reference, scratch it off of your "Daily" card and transfer the reference to a day-of-the-week card. Now every Monday, carry this day-of-the-week card along with your daily card and review the verse you learned.

Place a new reference on your "Daily" card and start working on memorizing it. When you memorize your second verse, write that reference on your Tuesday card, and so on.

Step Three: Now label a set of cards for each day of the month. Number them from 1 through 31. Once you have three verses on each day of the week, give yourself a test. Recite each verse you have on each day. If you can do it without looking the verse up in your Bible, scratch that verse off the day of the week card and transfer the reference to a day of the month card. If you learned all the verses, you will have a reference on monthly cards numbered 1 through 18.

Keep this system going. You will be constantly working on memorizing new verses while you review the old ones you have learned. It will take a little while to get four or five verses on each day-of-the-month card. Once you do, these verses will be so well ingrained into your head that you will be able to start a set of brand-new cards.

This system is personal, convenient, inexpensive, rewarding, engaging, and effective. Give it a try. The Word of God is alive and applicable for whatever you are facing today. Get ready to be able to "hit" those issues with the Word that you have locked inside your heart.

D—Discuss the Word

One of the best ways to learn something is to talk it over or teach others. You've worked at studying the Word, obeyed the Word you've studied, and you've begun to commit it to memory so you can use it whenever you need to do so. Now it's time to move out. Discuss the Word with God and with others. We will go into more depth about discussing the Word with God in the final chapter, so let's concentrate here on discussing the Word with others.

In Christianese, discussing the Word with other people is called *witnessing*. We don't need a degree from a Bible college or ordination papers to witness. All that's necessary to witness is for you to tell someone else about the God of the Bible as revealed through His creative work and the life of Jesus Christ. The power of the Holy Spirit is in you to enable you to do this. Jesus is speaking in John 14:26 when He says, *"But the Counselor, the Holy Spirit, whom the Father will send in my name, will teach you all things and will remind you of everything I have said to you."*

Get excited about life with Jesus. Share that excitement just as you would news of a great sale, a job opportunity, or an amazing accomplishment. Jesus is the best thing that can ever happen to a person. If you need help staying on track while sharing, use a little booklet like the Four Spiritual Laws, originally published and distributed by Campus Crusade for Christ, Inc. This tract distills the plan of salvation down to four, easy-to-communicate points that anyone can understand. The booklet even includes a sample prayer for that person to say to cement the commitment to their life.

If you don't have a copy of the Four Spiritual Laws to read, use your Bible and take a person down the Roman Road. This is four Scriptures in the Book of Romans that lead a person to a decision point for Christ. The verses are Romans 3:23 (all have sinned), Romans 5:8 (Christ died for our sins), Romans 6:23 (the wages of sin is death; the gift of God is eternal life through Jesus), and Romans 10:9–10 (confess Jesus and be saved).

Also be encouraged to tell people your story. What has God done in your life? By sharing our story, we let others know this life with Christ is real, fulfilling, practical, and it works.

 Step Aside: Practice sharing your faith with someone.

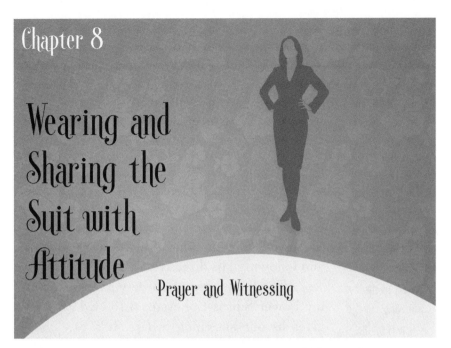

Chapter 8

Wearing and Sharing the Suit with Attitude

Prayer and Witnessing

OK, so we have on all the armor. We're all dressed up in our Power Suit. Now what? What exactly are we supposed to do in this getup? Live it up? Go forth and be blessed? Let everybody see how great we look in our armor?

No, a soldier gets dressed up in armor for one reason only—to do the work of a soldier, and that is to fight the enemy. Our enemies are Satan, the world, and our own flesh. We are to stand against the tricks of the devil (Ephesians 6:11), not love the world (1 John 2:15), and live by the Spirit and not the flesh (Galatians 5:18–25).

Our Power Suit is work clothes. We wear power suits in the business world to make an impression that says my company is on top of things, my company is in control. Our Power Suit represents us as executives in the kingdom of God. We are ambassadors sent to represent all the qualities of heaven. This suit enables us to be protected as we do the work God has called us to do. We're backed by the insurance of the company. We're always on company time—never off the clock. Our suit is recognizable by the competition. Even the color of a business power suit makes a statement: red making the most powerful statement. The red of our Power Suit is the blood of Jesus, the blood that is still effectively saving souls more than 2,000 years from the time it was originally spilt.

So the question still remains, "What am I supposed to do now that I'm all dressed in my Power Suit?" You face Satan and take your stand against him.

I submit to you that we are dressed in our godly work clothes in order to do the work of the kingdom. We do the work of the kingdom by staying in communication with our Leader and following His directives.

The final verse of our key passage about the Power Suit is Ephesians 6:18 (KJV). This gives us our marching orders. It says, *"Praying always with all prayer and supplication in the Spirit, and watching thereunto with all perseverance and supplication for all saints."* Basically, as long as we stay tuned in to God, we'll take our stand victoriously.

> Communication is key to the control of the battlefield of life.

So just how important is communication in war situations? Again, I turned to my brother Nick, the retired Marine Corps captain, in a quest to understand this point. He said, "Communications is the key to the control of the battlefield. The receiving of clear and prompt descriptions of the events transpiring on the front lines enables the commanders to make the timely decisions that will decide the success or failure of a mission. The clear dissemination of orders to the units on the line and the coordination of the support assets also have a direct effect on the success or failure on the battlefield. The real-time intelligence available and its timely dissemination to the battlefield commanders are crucial to the success of a mission."

So it is with spiritual warfare. Communication is key to the control of the battlefield of life. If we are not receiving clear and prompt descriptions of events transpiring, nor receiving our orders in a timely manner, the mission of our lives will end in disastrous defeat.

Prayer is communication with heaven. Ephesians 6:18 tells us we are to be involved in prayer, supplication, watching (being alert), and persevering.

Prayer: Prayer is simply communication with God that works throughout your life. It's a two-way conversation in which we must be careful to listen to what God wants us to know. He impresses His thoughts to you. You listen and you respond to Him. It's in the listening that you perceive how you are to respond. As I mentioned earlier, I like to write my prayers in a journal. These prayers include listening to God's thoughts because I write after I have read a passage of Scripture. I express to God what I feel, and discuss what He's saying to me through the passage and as applicable, commit to carry out His directive.

Make prayer a consistent aspect of your Christian life. Listen to what God says to you through His Word and in your mind and Spirit. If you've been out of communication, God's waiting with open arms for you to return.

> Make prayer a consistent aspect of your Christian life.

Supplication: The meaning of this older, lesser known word carries with it the idea of making requests on behalf of others. Our prayers no longer need to be exclusively focused just on ourselves. Now that we're dressed in the Power Suit, we will inevitably still talk to God about our personal needs, but we can move past mere personal maintenance into ministry. When my house is in order, I don't need to spend as much time on it. I'm free to help somebody else.

Step Aside: In order to remember all those for whom you want to pray, organize a prayer card system like the one I use. Separate your concerns into categories and assign each category to a day of the week. Mine are: Monday—myself and my husband; Tuesday—our children; Wednesday—ministries; Thursday—single people; Friday—married couples; Saturday—the unsaved. I rest on Sunday. In each category, each person or item has his, her, or its own card. On the card I write the name, the prayer concerns as they arise, and the answers as they happen. Then each day of the week, I pull out just that stack of cards and pray for the people or ministries in that group.

Watching: Watching has to do with keeping awake and being alert. A sleeping warrior on the battlefield is a dead warrior unless someone is keeping watch. First Peter 4:7 warns us, *"The end of all things is near. Therefore be clear minded and self-controlled so that you can pray."* Being watchful means we're alert to what's going on around us. There's not a lot of interference distracting our attention.

Pay attention to nuances, God's "still, small voice." Feed a hungry family tonight, provide a ride for someone trying to get to church, pay a struggling friend's phone bill, fill the tank of the person behind you in line at the gas station. A book entitled *Random Acts of Kindness* speaks of these. I call it listening to the voice of God for your fellow humans.

Persevering: Nelson's Bible Dictionary defines perseverance as "the steadfast effort to follow God's commands and to do His work. The New Testament makes it clear that faith alone can save. But it makes it equally clear that perseverance in doing good works is the greatest indication that an individual's faith is genuine." (See James 2:14–26.) *Unger's Bible Dictionary* says perseverance is an ethical term that "denotes the duty and privilege of a Christian to continue steadfastly in obedience and fidelity to Christ, not in order to inherit eternal life but to demonstrate love and gratitude to Christ for His great salvation."

As we speak with God and receive our directions from Him through prayer, send up supplications for others, remain alert, and stick to performing good works, we will be operating victoriously in our Power Suit, representing the kingdom well. My friend Donna sent me an example of a battlefield skirmish she encountered that exemplifies her implementation of all four of these elements—prayer, supplication, watching, and persevering. (I have emphasized each element so you won't miss them.)

> We will be operating victoriously in our Power Suit, representing the kingdom well.

In 2006 my godly husband stunned me when he walked away from our 13-year marriage. He was ugly in his actions, served me with divorce papers within weeks, and became someone I did not know. I was devastated and initially did not seek comfort in the Lord, but rather in an entire bottle of pills. God delivered me in such a way that still humbles me to this day. He audibly whispered my name and brought me back to Himself.

*In that moment of forgiveness I began truly to serve God for the first time. I studied, immersed myself in **constant prayers** (prayer) of deliverance for myself and my husband. I glowed at a time that was truly terrible. I stood by my husband despite his objections and vehement anger. **I prayed for him** (supplication) and refused to respond to the divorce papers. My loved ones and friends thought I had lost my mind. I guess I had in a way. I lost my mind and **replaced it with the mind of Christ** (watching). **I remained steadfast and trusted** (perseverance) the Lord's counsel alone.*

Two months later, my husband returned to his first love and shortly thereafter returned to our home. Since then, he has been seeking God first in all things. Our marriage has truly become God's, and my husband and I are best friends as Christ intended us to be. Praise be to God! We two have become one and been delivered by His grace and mercy.

Ladies, wear the Power Suit with purpose. Take off all the junk that causes the pieces not to fit. Wrap snugly into the good foundation garment of the belt of truth. Suit up in the breastplate of righteousness. Slip on the matching shoes of the preparation of the gospel of peace. Hold up the convertible, carryall shield of faith. Crown yourself with the helmet of salvation. Accessorize with the sword of the Spirit. And don't forget to pray. Dress up and move out!

Section 5
Reading Guide

Reading Power Suit

On Your Own or with a Group

$\mathcal{D}$ear Reader:

Power Suit: The Armor of God Fit for the Feminine Frame is designed to not only be read but also to be studied. Each "Step Aside" has been deliberately designed to assist you in your spiritual dressing room as you peel off the old clothes of your old ways and dress yourself snugly in the Power Suit, which is the armor of God.

If you are reading this book on your own, take each Step Aside seriously. I suggest using a journal dedicated only for this project in which you jot down your responses. You can then expand each of your Step Aside responses into a prayerful, conversational journal entry with God. Discuss with Him your thoughts and reactions. Look up and record in your journal additional cross-references from your Bible as you listen to God speak to you about each issue.

If you are reading this book as a group, use the Step Asides in each chapter as your discussion questions. The book can be covered as an eight-week course. The following reading guide will give you some suggestions. Open and close each classtime with prayer and have a great time "getting dressed."

Love,
Sharon

WEEK ONE—INTRODUCTION

Pass out the books to each participant.

Participants should also have a journal, spiral notebook, or pad of paper they intend to use only for their responses to this book. Consider supplying each person with a special journal, perhaps with the church's or group's name and logo on it, to make it special.

Introduce the book and the study for these eight weeks.

Read the introduction aloud.

Go around the group and ask each person to share what comes to mind when he or she thinks of spiritual warfare. There are no wrong answers. (If your class includes pastors, church leaders, or people who have attended Christian colleges or seminaries, let them share last so others won't feel intimidated.)

Now discuss the following questions:

1. What, if anything, do you already know about the armor of God?
2. What do you know about the devil?
3. Are you fearful of the devil? Why or why not?
4. Before reading any more of the book, do you think you can identify anything in your life you think is hindering the effectiveness of the armor of God?

Read chapter 1. Discuss each section briefly:

1. Ephesians 6:10–18
2. The Intention of the Power Suit
3. The Operation of the Power Suit
4. The Composition of the Power Suit

End your reading with "One Final Word in Review."

Assign
End the evening by giving the assignment to read chapter 2: "Good Foundation Garments: The Belt of Truth." Suggest that each person complete the five Step Asides in the chapter as they will be the basis of the discussion the next time you come together.

WEEK TWO — CHAPTER 2 — "GOOD FOUNDATION GAR-MENTS: THE BELT OF TRUTH"

Discuss
Ask the group their initial reactions or comments concerning the four spiritual certainties listed on page 33.

Talk through the chapter's five Step Asides.
Some of the answers can be very personal and penetrating, so suggest that your group discussions remain confidential. No one must share, but openness, honesty, and transparency is helpful for spiritual growth. Proverbs 27:17 (NKJV) says, *"As iron sharpens iron, so a man sharpens the countenance of his friend."*

After going through all the Step Asides, ask the class what they will take away from this chapter. They should realize that the Bible is the inerrant word of God and every command is meant to be — and can be — obeyed. Belief in and acceptance of anything other than truth blocks the fit of the belt of truth.

WEEK THREE — CHAPTER 3 — "SUITED UP: THE BREAST-PLATE OF RIGHTEOUSNESS"

Talk through the ten Step Asides for this chapter.
After going through all the Step Asides, ask the group what they will take away from this chapter. Among other things, the group should realize that the heart is the center of their being.

It is corrupted, injured, and destroyed by unrighteousness but protected by righteousness.

WEEK FOUR—CHAPTER 4—"SHOES TO MATCH: FEET SHOD WITH THE PREPARATION OF THE GOSPEL OF PEACE"

Talk through the four Step Asides of this chapter.
After going through all the Step Asides, ask the group what they will take away from this chapter. The group should realize that the shoes represent their trust in God as He is the only one who can adequately and successfully guide us through this life.

WEEK FIVE—CHAPTER 5—"CONVERTIBLE CARRYALL: THE SHIELD OF FAITH"

Discuss the breakdown of the verse starting on page 114.

Talk through the seven Step Asides of this chapter.
After going through all the Step Asides, ask the group what they will take away from this chapter. Among other things, the group should understand that *"faith is being sure of what we hope for and certain of what we do not see"* (Hebrews 11:1). *"Without faith it is impossible to please God"* (Hebrews 11:6). Behind the shield, we see God work.

WEEK SIX—CHAPTER 6—"CROWNING: HELMET OF SALVATION"

Talk through the six Step Asides of this chapter.
After going through all the Step Asides, ask the group what they will take away from this chapter. The group should see the necessity for a saving knowledge of Jesus Christ. Be sensitive to anyone who may be unsure of her salvation and share with her how she can be sure.

WEEK SEVEN — CHAPTER 7 — "JUST THE RIGHT ACCESSORY: THE SWORD OF THE SPIRIT, THE WORD OF GOD"

Talk through the first three Step Asides of this chapter.
Have extra copies of the Scheduling Work Sheet available and go over this together as a group.

Also, have index cards available so the group can build their Scripture memory system.

Ask the group what they will take away from this chapter. Among other truths, the group should grasp the importance of consistent study and reliance upon the Word of God as revealed in the Bible.

Discuss the final Step Aside. Talk through ways to naturally steer a conversation toward talking about the Lord. Practice with each other and then give the homework assignment to share your faith with someone new between now and the next meeting.

WEEK EIGHT — CHAPTER 8 — "WEARING AND SHARING THE SUIT WITH ATTITUDE: PRAYER AND WITNESSING"

Ask the group to share the experiences they had since the last meeting with sharing their faith. No stories can be shared of a time of sharing their faith that happened before the last meeting.

Discuss the four aspects of prayer:
Prayer, supplication, watching, and persevering.

Talk through the one Step Aside of this chapter.
Have index cards available and have each participant make his or her own prayer system.

After going through all the Step Asides, ask the group what they will take away from this chapter. The group should understand the importance of prayer and the excitement of witnessing in the life of a Christian.

Use the QR reader on your
smartphone to visit us online at
www.newhopepublishers.com

If you've been blessed by this book, we would like to hear your story. The publisher and author welcome your comments and suggestions at: newhopereader@wmu.org.

$\mathcal{D}$ear Reader:

Thank you for reading *Power Suit* and welcome to Life That Matters Ministries, a Christian organization that exists to encourage you to discover your life purpose and live up to your full potential. I want my life to count and I know you want yours to make a difference as well. I therefore encourage you to think biblically, speak intelligently, work passionately, act responsibly, love unconditionally, and most of all, live significantly. The five facets of this ministry will help you achieve these goals. Join in as we consider *"how we may spur one another on toward love and good works"* (Hebrews 10:24 NIV).

Sending you love that matters,
Sharon Norris Elliott,
Author and LTMM Founder and CEO

Life That Matters Ministries can help you:

• Discover your significant place in God's kingdom
• Grow in your faith
• Understand the Word of God, the Bible
• Study the Bible for yourself
• Develop a closer walk with the Lord
• Launch your writing career
• Plan your next women's retreat

The Life That Matters Ministries Web site is:
www.LifeThatMatters.net.

To contact the author with comments about the book, write to:
Life That Matters Ministries, P. O. Box 1519, Inglewood, CA 90308

To follow Sharon's blog, *A Heart for the Word*, log in to
www.sanewriter.wordpress.com

Other New Hope books for Women

BE RESTORED!
God's Power for African American Women
Debra Berry
ISBN-13: 978-1-59669-007-3

CERTAIN WOMEN CALLED BY CHRIST
Biblical Realities for Today
Paige Lanier Chargois
ISBN-13: 978-1-59669-200-8

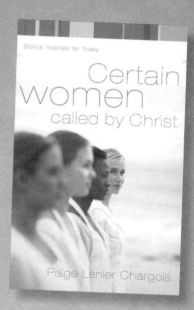

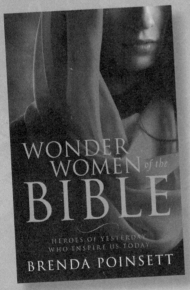

WONDER WOMEN OF THE BIBLE
Heroes of Yesterday Who Inspire Us Today
Brenda Poinsett
ISBN-13: 978-1-59669-094-3

Available in bookstores everywhere.

For information about these books or any New Hope product,
visit www.newhopepublishers.com.